What some are saying about... *Where are the Instructions?*

Thank you, Charles, for sharing so many experiences that were not only occasions of encouragement and hope for you, but experiences that can help so many others to know the peace and confidence that comes from a deep personal relationship with Christ. This is a wonderful little book!

Bishop Michael J. Sheridan, Catholic Diocese of Colorado Springs

This book contains nuggets of truth wrapped in stories that warm the heart, inspire the soul and draw from personal encounters as only my friend and colleague, Charles Castle, can share. Expect to be touched many times in equally many ways – perhaps even changed – as you uncover your own perspectives through these timeless stories.

D. Wendal Attig, Author, Speaker, and Online Reputation Marketing Consultant

WHERE ARE THE INSTRUCTIONS? identifies and shares the importance of 'story' in our everyday lives. 'Story' brings color back into our lives and enables us to identify key life lessons to learn and grow from"

Rich Griffith, Pastor, Woodmen Valley Chapel, Colorado Springs, Colorado

Charles, I am reading your book and it is just confirmation to me that you are in our lives for a reason. I am enjoying (sometimes with a few tears) your stories made more poignant by knowing you. Your life is a gift, thank you for sharing it with others.

Diane Rienstra, Montgomery, Texas

Charles Castle's short stories of his life experiences with people have inspired and reinforced my beliefs and other principles. The more I read, the more I realize that I need to listen more and be more compassionate in my interactions with others."

Larry Dyer, Colorado Springs, CO

"You have so much to share; it's so awesome you found a way to share it!"

Kandice Husarik, Schaumburg, Illinois

My friend Charles was kind enough to share his stories with me one by one as they were written before being compiled in this book. With humor, feeling and inspiration, Charles shares real life experiences from his heart."

Randy P. Geving, CIC, AAI Six & Geving Insurance, Inc.

"These stories didn't start as a book. They're simply slices of the author's life. Each story comes complete with a verse or passage from the Bible, and is an expression of the author's desire to live in light of it every day—and to help others do the same. In this spirit, may these stories touch your heart and inspire you to take to heart the life lessons that emerge with the telling of each one."

Dean Ridings Author, *The Pray! Prayer Journal*
Representative, The Navigators, Colorado Springs, Colorado

Where are the Instructions?

Short Stories
of Encouragement & Hope

Charles H. Castle

STEPHEN F. AUSTIN STATE UNIVERSITY PRESS
NACOGDOCHES, TEXAS

ISBN 978-1-62288-176-5

For more information:
Stephen F. Austin State University Press
P.O. Box 13007 SFA Station
Nacogdoches, Texas 75962
sfapress@sfasu.edu
www.sfasu.edu/sfapress
936-468-1078

Distributed by Texas A&M University Press Consortium
www.tamupress.com

Cartoon for The Christmas Card story is used with permission by
©Kimberly-Clark Worldwide, Inc.

Charles H. Castle may be reached at CharlesCastle07@gmail.com
or www.inspirationfortheheart.com

For my wife, Sherma.
What a blessing she's been to me with her
patience, kindness, and steadiness – *she's the love of my life!*

ACKNOWLEDGMENTS

I appreciate the counsel and direction of Dean Ridings with The Navigators and encouragement from Rich Griffith, Men's Minister at Woodmen Valley Chapel in Colorado Springs. I am thankful for ideas for these non-fiction short stories from the men in my weekly Thursday morning Bible study and from many men in fellowship on Tuesday mornings at our church. Thank you also to Bill Burd, good friend and author of *I Don't Care About your Resume*. A special thanks to my friend, T.J. McGinty, for his biblical knowledge in editing the book's Preface, enthusiasm for life and seeking the heart of God. T.J. passed away in 2015 and is in heaven with his Lord and Savior, Jesus Christ.

For every copy of *Where are the Instructions?* that's purchased, a portion of the profits will be given to Springs Rescue Mission (SRM). This long-standing local association is located at 5 W. Las Vegas Street, Colorado Springs, CO 80903, 719.632.1822, www. SpringsRescueMission.org, info@SpringsRescueMission.org. Springs Rescue Mission is a 501(c)3 nonprofit organization with Federal ID#: 84-1340824.

SRM's Vision: To see lives transformed and filled with hope as our community works together to fight homelessness, poverty and addiction. Their Mission: Because of our love for and obedience to God, our mission is to mobilize the community to provide relief, rehabilitation and empowerment services. SRM follows Matthew 25:35-36. For a listing of the 300 rescue missions located in North America, go to the Association of Gospel Rescue Missions at www. agrm.org.

CONTENTS

Introduction ⌐ 1

Preface ⌐ 3

Introspection ⌐ 5

The Howard P. Castle Canoe ⌐ 7
Canoeing is a sport, tradition and symbol of tranquility to me.

The Sign ⌐ 11
Some words, lumped together on a sign in my study, have inspired many ideas for my short stories. This is one of them!

Waiting 29 Years ⌐ 14
Going to a high school reunion, I heard some unexpected words and the positive impact of something I did when I was 10 years old.

Giving a Pint of Blood ⌐ 17
My parents rarely told me about their difficulties or health challenges. I learned to listen for clues of questions to ask.

I Can Either Go into Depression or Laugh ⌐ 20
My friend, Robert, used to believe he was a self-made man, could do anything himself and didn't need anybody's help.

The Missing Piano ⌐ 25
Being productive, creative and challenged is important. When time seems to be in slow motion, work is too routine and things are in a rut – I've looked for creativity in some interesting ways.

Tough Love ⌐ 28
It was a gradual transition from just being my mother's son to becoming her long-distance caregiver. Many of my decisions affected her health, independence and quality of life.

Sidewalk Address ⌐ 31
Seeing there was an untouched box of pizza remaining after an event, I asked about taking the box and giving it away. Then, upon driving into our inner city that's fraught with the roaming homeless, I looked to bless someone for their dinner that night.

Life is Full of Choices ✍ 35

*A son remembers his father as tough, scrappy, entrepreneurial and one of
the best World War II soldiers of our greatest generation.*

Where are the Instructions? ✍ 38

*In visiting our home, our five-year-old grandnephew was curious about an old
grandfather mantle chime clock resting on the floor next to my study.*

Shifting Gears ✍ 41

*Facing the reality of my depression is really about swallowing my pride,
asking for help and adjusting.*

The Christmas Card ✍ 45

*Having the Christmas spirit all year round gives me the opportunity to give
to others and encourage people. It has been a blessing!*

Expect the Most! ✍ 49

*In learning about the challenges of a young lady working behind a sandwich
shop counter, I decided to let God influence my decisions to make some
positive differences in her life.*

She Only Asked for Prayer ✍ 54

*Filling in the blanks for a young single mother was an honor. I watched her
Christian faith in action as she prayed, requested prayer and depended on
God for the results.*

The Homeless Man ✍ 59

*Being the same person to everyone – open, transparent and not hypocritical –
is much easier said than done.*

Where'd You Come From? ✍ 62

*Watching a lady fish through her credit cards and listening to her questions
to a deli shop manager, I believed she was hungry and looking for the cheapest thing on their menu.*

You Can Pray for Me ✍ 65

*In affirming a Church official in his stand on a controversial world issue,
I came to know what really mattered to him.*

Dear Dad ✍ 68

*My father said some harsh words to my wife while she was visiting my
parents. When my wife returned home she told me about the confrontation
and how hurt she felt. I pondered my words and six weeks later mailed him
this letter.*

No Bitterness in Your Heart ☞ 71

In a difficult situation, God showed me that praying for an organization and its members was better than becoming bitter towards them.

Presbyterian Gentleman ☞ 74

In fleeting moments, I will make a gesture that reminds me of my father or will look in the mirror and see a likeness of him.

By Your Side ☞ 77

The gift of life is very precious. God gave me the opportunity to candidly and gently tell my father some positive things before his heart surgery.

Leading with Faith First ☞ 80

Then all my other decisions for relationships, in casting votes, practicing good business ethics, how I treat others and all the rest – follow second.

Three Is Not a Crowd ☞ 83

An insurance company's TV ads inspire people to copy their actors' actions, but not necessarily buy their products.

Integrity Has One Face ☞ 86

Dishonesty, deceit, omission of facts, lying and a myriad of other untruths, constitute fraud and are delivered with many faces.

Practicing Humor, Humility, and Heart ☞ 89

I am not a big fan of parking meters and believe they actually prevent and discourage business. Following are three examples of reactions to them.

Falling Into Place ☞ 93

On a hike with others, one slip could have resulted in injuries or worse. Instead, I walked away with only grass stains on my golf shirt.

Flunking Out of College ☞ 96

The path of obtaining my college degree taught me the value of having purpose, possessing confidence…and just moving forward.

Relationship Matters ☞ 100

An employer once announced in a sales meeting, "When you know people and don't use them, it's worthless." Not agreeing with his viewpoint, I do believe in utilizing relationships with a servant's heart – and that's worthwhile! A correlation to this was my privilege in getting to know a federal Congressman in the Houston area.

Tell Them the Truth Mark! ⁓ 104

While mentoring a man, I watched him shrink the gap between his old thinking and his new life in Christ.

Ever Stolen Anything? ⁓ 108

This question was asked on a Securities Exchange Commission questionnaire, and after some thought, I answered "Yes" with a short explanation.

After I'm Dead and Gone ⁓ 111

INTRODUCTION

In the mid-90s, I was training a sales representative to sell advertising for a church publication company. As he and I connected with the local church in Baytown, Texas, prospected for businesses, set appointments and did presentations – we had a lot of *"window time"* together. After a few days, he told me that my God-given gift was encouraging people. I have strived at fulfilling my gift since then!

I grew up in Beaumont and Dallas, Texas with loving parents and my younger sister. Dad was a lawyer – first as a lieutenant in the Army Air Force in World War II, later in private practice, then with an oil tool corporation and lastly in retirement doing pro bono cases for non-profits and for parents wanting to adopt children. Mom earned a degree in economics from the University of Alberta, became an American when she married Dad, worked at a company until I was five years old and then stayed home full time. Both of my parents volunteered for non-profits helping those less fortunate and were active in their church homes. My parents did not tell me much of the accolades of their avocations in serving others; I learned of their actions from their colleagues and friends. My mother prepared every meal except when we traveled to and from vacation destinations – it was years later that I learned she did not have a sense of smell.

Our family went to church every Sunday... I was active in Boy Scouts of America in Troop 70 in Dallas where I attained my Eagle Scout... school was pretty boring as I usually was a B and C student...paper routes and restaurant jobs were staples... participating and watching sports were not on my radar...and I began dating just before turning 17.

After high school graduation, I enrolled at Stephen F. Austin State University in Nacogdoches, Texas. That college stint lasted eight years – flunking out, working a while and graduating with a degree in Communications/Journalism and Political Science.

After college, my travels to Nacogdoches ran for another 33 years until my mother died there. My career has mostly been in selling intangible products like advertising and insurance while I dabbled some in writing. A few years ago, I wrote down a goal to finally publish these short stories into a book. That goal was accomplished!

I tell people I had to leave Texas to find a wife. Six weeks after graduation, I landed a job with a newspaper in Boulder, Colorado. Two weeks later, I met my wife, Sherma, at a Halloween party. We got engaged two months after that and married six months later. She's the love of my life!

The greatest asset I will ever own is my belief and faith in God and His Son, Jesus. I became a Christian in my mid-30s and I'm a work in progress until the day I die. My salvation is free – no costs, works to be done or IOUs to be fulfilled. I have debates and disagreements with God...and frankly my questions, His answers and forgiveness continue to develop our closer relationship and friendship. My Bible study friends and church men's group are weekly staples of stable Christians in my life. God often taps on my shoulder to befriend and relate to those who do not know Him and those that do. He has told me, *"Why would anyone be interested in your faith, if you treat them poorly or operate from your own pride?"* Take a look at Luke 3:1-6.

The format for each short story begins with its title and a description of why you may want to read it. Then the story is related with some detail and comes to the point quickly. At the end of each story is a Bible verse address with my conclusion. If you are interested in what the verse says, then look it up. On a separate page following each story are *Questions to Ponder?* These questions are not in order of priority for you to consider – only to give food for thought and to ask more questions.

My hope is that you, your family and friends will read *Where are the Instructions?* Pass your copy on to others. For copies that are sold, a percentage of the profits will be given to Springs Rescue Mission, a non-profit that we support in Colorado Springs.

May God bless and keep you,

Charles Castle

PREFACE

A few years ago my sister and only sibling died unexpectedly. It was the week before Christmas. I flew to Texas to be with our mother and stayed to attend the funeral and the activities of Christmas week. Each night Mom and I talked about the family. We remembered with fondness about my father, who had died seven years earlier, and now, my sister.

During our time together, I shared many stories with Mom and after each she would say, *"Charles, this story is really good. You ought to write it down!"* After I returned home from our visit, I wrote down more than 100 story ideas. A year later, I began to write the stories in greater detail. *Where are the Instructions?* is a result of those efforts—as well as editing and input from others who helped shape the book.

I wrote this collection of short stories so that my life experiences, challenges and praises, may inspire, encourage and give you hope. One of the most important things in my life is my Christian faith, and you will see God's hand woven into each story. At the end of each story, I've provided a correlating Bible verse with a personal comment, followed by some questions for you to think about.

First, it may be helpful to know how my faith journey began. As a child, I believed I was a saved Christian because I attended church, completed confirmation classes at age 12 and was good most of the time. However, I didn't have a relationship with God until my mid-30s.

One afternoon, in a friend's office, I prayed to receive Jesus Christ as my Savior. I prayed to God to receive peace, forgiveness of my sins, and abundant, eternal life. One of the Bible verses that inspired me was Ephesians 2:8-9, *"For it is by grace you have been saved, through faith—and this is not from yourselves, it is the gift of God—not by works, so that no one may boast."* Other essential Scripture verses were Romans 10:9: *"That if you confess with your mouth the Lord Jesus and believe in your heart that God raised Him from the dead, you will be saved."*…I John 5:11-13: *"And this is the testimony: that God has given us eternal life, and this life is in His Son. He who has the Son has life; he who does not have the Son of God does not have life. These things I have written to you who believe in the name of the Son of God, that you may know that you have eternal life, and that you may continue to believe in the name of the Son of God."*...Revelation 3:20: *"Behold, I stand at the door and knock. If anyone hears My voice and opens the door, I will come and dine with him, and he with Me."*

When I was a new believer, I went on a sales call to sell an advertisement to a plumber. The man asked me, *"Would you be interested in a men's Bible study?"* Thinking it was part of the sale I said, *"Yes."* The plumber bought the ad, and I never saw him again. On the way back to the office, I looked at the card he had given me; it listed 10 Bible studies. So I called the contact person for the study that met closest to my home and began attending the group every Thursday morning.

Three months into the Bible study, we had a death in our family. Tragically, Bob Ely, my wife's uncle and the minister who married us, was murdered in a robbery. At the Bible study that week, the men helped me understand more about God's sovereignty in the context of that tragedy. During that time, my faith was deepened. When the Bible study leader offered to disciple and mentor me in my Christian faith, I accepted. We met weekly or bi-weekly for three years to study God's Word and find application in our lives.

Today my faith is on fire for God! He knows everything I say and do—and when I ask, He forgives my transgressions and gives me direction for my life. When I die, I believe God will have some questions for me. One will be, *"Did you believe in my Son, Jesus, that He died and rose again?"* I will confidently answer, *"Yes,"* because of His promise of salvation, and my name is in His Book of Life. He will then ask me about how I spent my time, talents and treasure to evangelize unbelievers and edify the body of Christ. My answers may determine how I spend eternity in heaven with Him. I am glad to say that my Christian faith is the greatest asset I will ever own!

As you read this collection of stories from my life and the lives of others, it is my hope these stories will encourage, inspire and *warm your heart*!

God bless you,

Charles H. Castle

INTROSPECTION

Years ago, when I did not have a relationship with God and His Son, Jesus Christ, I believed Christians were weak; they had no fun and were hypocrites. Because of that, I would challenge their faith or I'd put up an emotional wall so they could not penetrate my unbelief.

After becoming a Christian in my mid-30s, I learned my ideas about Christian believers were not always true. I also discovered that many people had been praying for God to reach my heart and to change me. And when I came to know the Lord in a life-changing way, He impressed upon me to be open and frank about my faith— and certainly not be a hypocrite. God asked me to share His truth in love by doing E^2 – evangelism x edification. His question has been, *"Why would anybody have an interest in your Christian faith if you treat them poorly or were not real with them?"*

I aim to treat others well and be honest with them. And, when I make mistakes, *and I do every day*, I am grateful that God forgives me. He leads me with His Holy Spirit (Galatians 5:18-26). My prayer is to finish well and remain **FAT** — **F**aithful, **A**vailable and **T**eachable. As I make plans, I ask God to lead my steps. He is in charge of the results!

At the conclusion of each story, I have drawn some conclusions. Perhaps you might consider them and other ideas for discussion with friends, a book club or in your prayers.

When Jay Leno was the host of *The Tonight Show*, I listened to his monologues regularly. I learned more about what was going on in the world from his satire and comments than from any other media. Leno is a master of entertaining and informing at the same time. For you, I think of these short stories as a way of entertaining, giving ideas to ponder and laughing a little, too!

Whether you are in a spiritual quest, searching for answers in this crazy world, need God's comfort or want inspiration, I believe you'll enjoy reading these short stories.

Blessings to you,

Charles H. Castle

THE HOWARD P. CASTLE CANOE

Canoeing is a sport, tradition and symbol of tranquility to me.

After my father retired, my parents stayed for weeks each summer at the Castle Point cabin in Waupaca, Wisconsin. They always rented canoes, but now that they were spending more time on the Chain 'O Lakes, my parents purchased a canoe. My father, Howard P. Castle, named the canoe after himself, or perhaps for his father since Dad was Howard P. Castle, Jr.

The canoe was well-constructed, with good buoyancy. It rarely tipped and was great for bobbing. Canoeing was a ritual for my father as he self-propelled the canoe across Beasley Lake. My mother and father would take their canoe out and paddle to the upper and lower chains, Emmons Creek, Hartman's Creek and Beasley Creek. Dad was broad-shouldered and physically fit, with tan, bronzed skin from the summer sun. He always canoed in the stern and I learned the skill and sport from him.

There were only three times the canoe was paddled for less-happy occasions. The first time was for a family emergency. One morning my father's youngest brother, Arthur, was swimming alone in the lake just past the square dock. Suddenly, Arthur had a heart attack and drowned before anyone could reach him. My father was swimming with my mother on the other side of the lake and was the first to arrive. He tried CPR on my uncle, but with no success. When the EMTs arrived they could not revive Arthur either. The slope up the stairs from the lake to the cabin was too steep for the ambulance gurney to transport Arthur's body. So the medical team and my father placed his body in the Howard P. Castle canoe, while the rest of the family watched. Dad then paddled across Beasley, Long and Columbia lakes to port at Indian Crossing to meet the ambulance.

The second time, the canoe was used to distribute my father's ashes on Beasley Lake. He had passed away earlier in the winter and Mom, my sister, Keltie, and I flew to Chicago in June for the drive north to Waupaca. Dad's ashes were mailed via UPS in a paper urn and had arrived earlier to the bed and breakfast inn where we stayed.

As we checked in, the inn owner said the box was delivered with a hole in it. I did not tell him then the contents were my father's ashes...or that Dad had been "distributed" from Nacogdoches, Texas to Waupaca! I took the box back to our rooms, and that night we attempted to scoop the ashes back into the urn; it was odd sifting through Dad's remains.

The next morning we headed to the rustic cabin which was built by Dad's father in the 1920s. We walked down the stairway to Beasley Lake where other family members had prepared the Howard P. Castle canoe for our trip. Dad had started going to the lakes when he was just seven years old. Keltie sat in the bow, Mom positioned herself in the center with Dad's urn and I steered the canoe in the stern. We pulled away from the dock to find a place to dedicate Dad's ashes in the 50-foot-deep lake.

Keltie and I paddled the canoe in silence. It was very quiet and still; there were no other boats on the lake. I sensed an edge in the air since what we were doing was so final. We found a calm spot in about 20 feet of water – it was so clear we could see the bottom of the lake with the glint of the morning sun.

My sister placed the urn on the water expecting it to slowly dissolve, but it unexpectedly—and quickly—sank to the bottom! The punctured hole made it sink like a lead balloon. The three of us sat with our mouths agape. Mom said, *"Gee, your father was funny to the last!"* We stayed a short time and then paddled to Beasley Creek to spread some of Dad's ashes there. Then we canoed to a wildlife refuge, Emmons Creek, to spread the last of his ashes.

We flew home the next day. My mother visited the cabin and Beasley Lake two more times before she died.

The third time the canoe was used to distribute my mother's ashes in Beasley Lake. My cousin, Dave, was in the bow while I paddled in the stern. We went out to the same place where we had put Dad's urn on the water while my Castle cousins watched from the square dock. Then, I said a prayer for my mother. As I was emptying her ashes in the lake, a gust of wind came up and blew a lot of the ashes into the canoe! It seemed God has a sense of humor and the levity was certainly welcomed that late summer afternoon.

The Howard P. Castle canoe is still at the cabin and we reserve it for our family reunions. Whenever I visit Waupaca and our cabin, I take the Howard P. Castle canoe out for a solo trip. I can feel Dad's presence as I paddle the lake.

When I read II Corinthians 1:3-5, God comforts me
as I do uncomfortable and difficult things.
I am thankful my father taught me the sport of
canoeing and is watching over me always.

QUESTIONS TO PONDER?

✳   *Do I fear death – why or why not?*

✳   *When I think about the deceased people I loved,*
what do I remember first and best about them?

My Notes:

THE SIGN

Some words, lumped together on a sign in my study, have inspired many ideas for my short stories. This is one of them!

After my mother passed away just before Christmas a few years ago, my wife and I drove to her memorial service in early January. It's a 1,000-mile one-way trip from Colorado Springs to Nacogdoches, Texas. Many family members came to her memorial service from South Texas, New Mexico, Connecticut and two from Canada. It was a joyous occasion! The four days were a whirlwind of emotions, necessary things to do and saying goodbye to many of Mom's friends I'll probably never see again. One of my future short stories will be *When in Nacogdoches*, and it'll cover five decades of my visits and college years there. I have many fond memories of both, especially since my parents retired there after my college stints.

On our return trip home from Mom's memorial service, we drove through the little town of Chillicothe, Texas (pop. 686) that's northwest of Fort Worth. It's an old-looking town that loses about 5% of its population every census. Besides the Dairy Queen, Chillicothe has one store that Sherma and I always like to visit. I don't remember the name of the store; it's a knick-knack place that also sells pecans when they're in season. Fortunately, the store was still open, as it was 4:30 and not 5 p.m., closing time. We bought some already-cracked pecans and looked around at the rest of their merchandise.

I then saw a sign that read, *"Faith is not knowing what the future holds but knowing who holds the future."* I liked the sign's words, but wrestled about paying $26 for it. Then my emotions took over...I realized this was our last trip through Chillicothe... and the sign's words had a special meaning for me. I gave in and bought the sign! It sits on the window ledge in my study and I read its words a few times every day. And those words have inspired the ideas and oomph of many of my short stories.

In reading Romans 1:17 and Psalm 119:30, I have hope for the future.

QUESTIONS TO PONDER?

✽   *Do you put hope in things and people – like the place you live, your job, friends or what?*

✽   *If your job transferred you to a smaller or larger city – what changes would it make on you and your family?*

✽   *Do you think people are different that live in small towns versus larger cities?*

✽   *What does faith mean to you?*

✽   *What are some little things that have had a big impact on your life?*

✽   *What are some of your favorite sayings, Bible verses, people to be around, books and audios? Why and how do they inspire you?*

My Notes:

WAITING 29 YEARS

Going to a high school reunion, I heard some unexpected words and the positive impact of something I did when I was 10 years old.

I received an invitation to attend my 20th high school reunion. Since I had only been to a fraternity reunion 10 years before, I was a bit reluctant in going. Then I called a friend, Kevin, who went to high school and Boy Scouts with me to see if he was going, too. He said, *"Yes,"* and offered for me to stay in his home while we both went to the reunion.

For the round trip from Houston to Dallas I took the train. The six-hour ride each way meandered through the small towns' backsides revealing their poorer neighborhoods. All of my other trips were by car via I-45 that showcased their better-looking buildings. The train was unique and fun – though I did not repeat that experience again.

After the six-hour train ride, I arrived at the downtown Dallas station and rented a car. Then, I visited the old neighborhood where I grew up in University Park, got a haircut at the familiar barbershop in Snyder Plaza and dropped in to see some old friends. Afterwards, I drove to Kevin's home that was located in a newer Dallas suburb.

The Friday evening party was a big drunk – lots of people were attempting to impress others with their accomplishments since our high school graduation. I connected with some of the people I knew, and found it to be an odd experience.

Saturday afternoon's event was a picnic in the park across from the police station. Then we all went on a *"guided tour"* through the high school building. To this day I still have memories of walking those halls and dreading school classes. I was a "C" student who did not participate in school activities much. My extracurricular work was in Scouting, as I attained my Eagle badge, and attended church youth programs.

The Saturday night party was at a hotel on Central Expressway. The same people who got drunk on Friday night were getting drunk again. We were given tags that had our senior pictures and printed names on them. In approaching people I found myself doing double-takes – looking at their name tag to recognize who was standing in front of me.

As I came in the front door of the hotel, a lady approached me. As I looked at her name tag, she had not changed at all in appearance in 20 years. She said, *"Hi, Charles – I'm glad you are here. I've been waiting a long time to tell you something."* I winced with the thought, *"Uh, oh, I wonder what she's going to say?"*

Her name was Lysa. I remember going to grade school, junior high and high school with her. She was always tall in stature and had a quiet spirit about her. Lysa had become a nurse and that occupation fit her caring demeanor and attitude. Lysa said, *"When my parents moved to Dallas I was in the 4th grade…they enrolled me in Miss Heron's class at University Park Elementary. You were in class with me and were the only person who befriended me. And, you made it possible for me to get through that year. I was hoping you would come to this reunion so I could thank you and tell you how much your friendship meant to me."*

I felt very humble and stumbled with, *"You're welcome."* Lysa had waited 29 years to give me this thank-you. Her words gave me a timeline…of what my personality was like when I was nine-years-old turning 10. Lysa's thank-you made my reunion trip all worthwhile – what a treat it was to hear her kind words!

In reading Ezekiel 36:23, my prayer is
that I lead with the Holy Spirit
and not of myself.

QUESTIONS TO PONDER?

❧   *How can I show loving kindness in my speech and actions toward others?*

❧   *For the people who know you the best – how would they describe your character and demeanor?*

❧   *What does being a Pharisee mean to you?*

❧   *What experiences – good, mediocre and bad – have you had at an alumni event? Will you go to another one? Would you invite your spouse, fiancée or a special person?*

My Notes:

GIVING A PINT OF BLOOD

My parents rarely told me about their difficulties or health challenges.
I learned to listen for clues of questions to ask.

I learned about my father's prostate cancer during a phone call from my mother. Dad was having the surgery the next day in Nacogdoches, 140 miles from our home in Houston. The next morning, I drove Highway 59 north to Nacogdoches, buying seven newspapers along the way.

Nacogdoches has two hospitals and Dad's surgery was scheduled for the one closest to downtown. As I was nearing the hospital, I noticed the blood bank was located right in front of the hospital. I had not given blood since fainting in a failed attempt 20 years earlier! So, I thought, *"It's time to break the cessation on giving blood, and honor my father."* The nurses told me there was not enough time to screen my blood for his surgery, since it was a 120-mile turnaround to and from Tyler, Texas. To my surprise, I was successful in giving a pint of blood *and* not fainting!

After giving the blood, I walked into the surgery waiting area and found my mother. Her comment startled me with, *"I hope it's a long operation."* If the surgeon determined the cancer was too advanced, the operation would be cut short. Dad would be then sewn up with the hope of living only a few months. It was a wonderful blessing that the surgery lasted three *l-o-n-g* hours! Each of the seven newspapers I had purchased earlier, had a different crossword puzzle in it. Together, Mom and I methodically filled out each one. As we were finishing up the last puzzle, the doctor came in and said Dad was being wheeled into a recovery room. His cancer operation was a success!

Soon afterwards, I took Mom to lunch. A few hours later, Dad was moved to a private room. And, we visited Dad several times that weekend.

As I was preparing to leave Nacogdoches on Sunday afternoon, I went by the hospital to visit Dad. He said with his dry sense of humor, *"I'm pretty squirrelly now — I've got your pint of blood in me.*" During the night Dad had some internal bleeding. Fortunately, the blood bank had marked my pint of blood with top priority and it was screened quickly for Dad's use.

When I was six weeks old, Dad gave me a pint of blood for an emergency operation. Now 40 years later, I was giving it back.

In reading Luke 6:38 and II Corinthians 9:7, giving and receiving are best measured in God's terms, not mine.

QUESTIONS TO PONDER?

✻   *What are you willing to give up or sacrifice to benefit a friend or family member?*

✻   *Do family and friends tell you what's really going on with serious issues?*

✻   *What do you fear and why do you fear it?*

✻   *Every heard of or been to Nacogdoches, Texas? With your eyes closed, can you pronounce and spell Nacogdoches correctly?*

My Notes:

_____

_____

_____

_____

_____

_____

_____

_____

_____

_____

_____

_____

_____

_____

_____

_____

_____

I CAN EITHER GO INTO DEPRESSION
OR LAUGH

My friend, Robert, used to believe he was a self-made man, could do anything himself and didn't need anybody's help. He then made some bad choices in his construction business resulting in an Internal Revenue Service criminal investigation of filing two false tax statements. It nearly cost him a 20-30 year prison sentence and a $530,000 tax assessment.

Robert asked me to write his story and the notes for it were taken in his home. He and his wife, Sharon, have been married for 54 years, raised two children, served on mission trips to Russia...*and* have a resume of life experiences.

Robert has led a full life! Now, in his 80s, his accomplishments include serving in the armed forces, earning undergraduate/master degrees while paying his own way, running construction businesses and staying strong in his Christian faith. I believe he *"married up"* to Sharon who has stuck with him through the thick and the thin. Their marriage is truly what it means to serve God and each other, *"For better or worse!"*

He became a Christian at age nine with the confession of making Jesus Christ as Lord of his life. Baptism, membership and staying out of trouble followed with a church in Denver, Colorado. At Denver University, he tried out for cheerleading and ended up being the mascot, Pioneer Pete. In his early career years, Robert aimed at the goal to become a millionaire before turning 30. He was given some opportunities by an older businessman to design and build houses for people. His first closing netted him a negative $500, while only having a nickel in his pocket. A broker, at the transaction, cut his commission so Robert came out even. Though, it was a rough start, he was determined to become an independent and successful businessman.

During the 1960s, his construction business thrived and many investors were interested in his projects. One of these men was a future governor of Colorado and others thought Robert's work ethic and return-on-investment business plans were top notch! A volunteer organization, Full Gospel Business Men International (FGBMI), appointed him as a youth director one year. He began to believe he was self-made with autonomy and control. Still active in the church where he and Sharon met, Robert began to see business as more important...than his relationship with God.

Robert was not asked to do another volunteer term for FGBMI. He then wrote off the organization, but continued to stay active in the Church. He gradually ebbed away from associating with men and women of his Christian faith and began spending more time with pagans. Because his business was failing, Robert then filed for bankruptcy. But, with his entrepreneurial spirit, he developed some new construction projects that increased his income.

A few years later, after being approached by a known associate and now an employee of a chain business, Robert entered into an arrangement with that employee. After projects were bid by other construction companies, the employee communicated to Robert the number of the lowest bid. He then underbid the number...and was awarded the contract. He then paid a $10,000 fee to the employee. In the beginning, both men agreed their arrangement was wrong. But, after the third deal, they rationalized because no one was hurt and they were saving the company money, they continued their practice. The arrangement lasted for three years until the employee was abruptly transferred to another position. A few years after their arrangement ended, the Internal Revenue Service (IRS) began an investigation into Robert's tax returns.

After a couple of years of grueling interviews and hiring an attorney to defend him, Robert was indicted with two counts of falsifying tax returns. In being confronted by the IRS, Robert had the choice to own up to lying and his mistakes. He finally pled guilty to one charge and the IRS dropped the other one. His attorney said he'd be at least 70 years old before getting out of prison. In one of the meetings, Robert was waiting alone in a conference room. His attorney and the IRS prosecutor entered the room and declared, *"It looks like your tax liability is $530,000!"* Robert replied with a smile, *"I can either go into depression or laugh."*

Reasoning his life was over, Robert turned to God and asked Him, *"What is going on in my life?"* In prayer, the Lord revealed to him that his actions had been an abomination to God and he'd been living a phony Christian life. If Robert turned his life over to God, began reading the Bible again and worshipping Him, God would intervene on his behalf. Robert accepted God's intervention and The Lord then promised Robert he would not serve time in prison. He hoped God's promise would be a shortcut to deliver him from the investigation, too, but the arduous process lasted seven years. His attorney, probation officer and the IRS prosecutor all told him he was going to prison. The IRS suggested if Robert gave them the name of the associate of the business chain, his prison time would be nil and he'd possibly gain immunity. Robert replied, *"No, I can't do that,"* because God's promise was to him and didn't involve the associate. To date, he's never revealed the associate's name.

In Robert's new walk with God, he confessed his transgressions to all he met. He was under some house arrest time and wore his ankle bracelet for 3- 1/2 months. It became a conversation opener to his ordeal. As Robert relayed his story to an individual, his testimony abounded about God's intervention and saving grace. Forgiveness and restoration began to transform his life. Prayers were spoken by many over Robert and Sharon and the presiding sentencing judge. Robert's *Hearing on Sentencing the Reporter's Transcript* read in part, by his attorney: *"One of the most difficult things _(Robert)_ had to do throughout this whole scenario is face his wife of 29 years and admit to her what he had done, face his pastor, the people in church; the people with whom he is closest friends are the people in church, the people he lives with day in, day out, prays with, works with, involved in community projects with."* The judge told Robert that his crime dictated he had to serve some time in jail. But, the judge then said, *"Something inside of me, that I cannot explain, told me prison time for you would serve no purpose."* Though, the judge changed his mind five days later to incarcerate Robert, he then returned to his original conviction to not send him to prison.

A few years later, he attended an accountant's seminar, and became the professional's client. The accountant negotiated for a year with the IRS to reduce his back tax bill to $11,000, and he paid it quickly. Robert didn't go to prison, did not have or pay a tax liability and is still married to Sharon! I believe God rescued Robert...and He can do the same for you and me.

The following are two lessons Robert learned from his ordeal: *"I received 3-1/2 months of house detention with an ankle bracelet. At first, I tried to hide the bracelet, but God told me if I would not try to hide it, the bracelet would not become a problem. In those 3-1/2 months, I was able to use the bracelet as a witness tool about God's mercy, love and deliverance."*

"Years before (the ordeal), *Sharon and I developed a close friendship with Jim and Bonnie, who lived next door to* _ (the sentencing judge) _. *They walked around their house every day for God to send angels to minister to the judge. Bonnie's love and friendship made it possible for Sharon to stay* (with me) *that saved our marriage."*

Through his tribulation, Robert held on to the Bible verses of *II Corinthians 12:8-9, Luke 21:14-15 and Proverbs 26:11. May God bless and keep you as you go through trials and afflictions.*

QUESTIONS TO PONDER?

✳   *Since our tax system is based on individuals' honor, have you ever cheated or fudged on the numbers of your tax returns?*

✳   *Do you rationalize that doing a wrong is actually okay and acceptable?*

✳   *Have you ever been rescued from a tragedy, dilemma or problem? How did it make you feel?*

✳   *If you were in an ordeal like Robert's experience, where would you turn first?*

✳   *Would your spouse stay as your partner through an ordeal like Robert's?*

✳   *What does trusting God through an ordeal, tragedy or tribulation mean to you?*

✳   *What is important to you…and why?*

My Notes:

THE MISSING PIANO

Being productive, creative and challenged is important to me. When time seems to be in slow motion, work is too routine and things are in a rut – I've looked for creativity in some interesting ways.

While attending the summer sessions in college, I continued my capacity as advertising manager of *The Pine Log*, the college paper of Stephen F. Austin State University. After sending one of the editions to press, one of my friends, Mike, a photographer, and I were bored. We were watching one of the noon mini-concerts wind down on the plaza below.

It was a humid, 100-degree day and everyone scattered for the air conditioning when it was over. The maintenance crew was supposed to come by and pick up the upright piano and bench right afterwards. Since the crew didn't come for 30 minutes, we decided to enliven our boring day and have a little fun.

Mike and I nonchalantly walked onto the plaza, rolled the piano through the first floor doors of the Rusk Building and left the bench for the maintenance crew! About 10 minutes later, the crew arrived and we watched them look all over the plaza for that piano. They took the bench while we had a good laugh from the second floor. The crew reported the piano stolen to the university's police security.

Then a half hour later, we reported where the piano was and security sent the police chief to our newspaper office. He wanted to press charges – but the director of student publications asked him to accept our apology for *"poor judgment"* instead.

Our prank caused an all-points-bulletin to be dispatched for a missing piano and created a little havoc on that hot summer day. We went a little too far with our prank, but Mike and I still enjoy the memories.

In reading Ecclesiastes 9:10,
I hope I wisely use the time that I'm given!

QUESTIONS TO PONDER?

❋ *In my youth, I made some poor choices. Am I*
more mature in my thoughts and actions now?

❋ *How can I turn my intellect and creativity*
into useful and productive progress?

❋ *What are some outlets where I can use my talents*
to serve myself, family, others and God?

❋ *Who and what do I gain my significance from*
— people, work and/or focus of worship?

Printed in *The Sawdust Supplement*, Fall 1993, alumni publication of
Stephen F. Austin State University, Nacogdoches, Texas

My Notes:

TOUGH LOVE

*It was a gradual transition from just being my mother's son
to becoming her long-distance caregiver. Many of my decisions
affected her health, independence and quality of life.*

In the first week in October, my 84-year-old mother fell and broke her hip. Immediately, I left from Colorado Springs for the 1,000-mile driving trip to Nacogdoches, Texas. Around 2 a.m., I stopped at an old motel in Decatur, which is near Fort Worth. With four hours of sleep under my belt, I got back on Highway 287 and headed for Nacogdoches. Later that morning, Mom's doctor called me and said, *"Don't need to hurry, we can't do the surgery because her blood pressure is too low."*

When I arrived Friday afternoon to her hospital room, she was elated to see me...and Mom's blood pressure went up! The next morning she was hydrated with normal blood pressure and the surgery was done. She remained in the hospital, probably longer than the usual recovery time, because of her age. I spent a week in my college town staying at Mom's apartment and visiting her several times a day. The following Friday, she was transported by ambulance to the rehabilitation clinic across the street from the hospital. The arduous process of three weeks of physical therapy then began.

Since I had stayed much longer than expected, and she was now in rehab, I packed up my suitcase and made plans to leave Saturday morning. When I walked into the rehab clinic, Mom was in a wheelchair in the atrium next to the front entrance. After visiting with her a bit, I said, *"I'm leaving for home."* My mother begged me to stay, which made my departure very difficult.

My words were soft and direct with, *"Mom, I need you to work hard and do everything the physical therapists tell you to do. If you do the work diligently, you will go home to your assisted-living apartment. If not, you'll have to go to a nursing home."* She said, *"You've visited me almost every month this year...how can you take the time off to see me next month?"* I said, *"No matter where you are staying, we'll be here!"*

When my wife and I visited for Thanksgiving five weeks later, we saw Mom in her apartment. She successfully completed her physical therapy regimen and was elated to be home!

In reading II Timothy 3:16 and Matthew 7:12,
I believe my actions were done in love.

QUESTIONS TO PONDER?

❋ *Have you had a situation where tough love was needed…and how did you initially respond?*

❋ *How did the other person receive your discipline and "love?"*

❋ *Have you ever witnessed or done what a caregiver does for another person?*

❋ *Think about initiating something special for a caregiver – spelling them for a day, dinner treated by you and/ or a gift that would let them know they are loved.*

❋ *Do you have elderly parents and other loved ones who need your intervention? Have you engaged them in a future plan of action regarding their health care and other needs?*

My Notes:

_____

_____

_____

_____

_____

_____

_____

_____

_____

_____

_____

_____

_____

_____

_____

_____

_____

_____

_____

SIDEWALK ADDRESS

Seeing there was an untouched box of pizza remaining after an event,
I asked about taking the box and giving it away. Then, upon driving
into our inner city that's fraught with the roaming homeless,
I looked to bless someone for their dinner that night.

Three of Colorado Springs' community centers organize a 5k run for the last Friday of the summer months – June, July and August. For the June date, I did not go as a participant runner; though, I am optimistic about running in the July and August events. Since I represented one of the community centers for our volunteer parks board, I did some glad-handing to meet and greet the business sponsors, staff coordinating the event and the families who showed up. It was a lot of fun – and fortunately it didn't rain and there weren't any lightning strike scares. After the runners finished the race, the staff offered water, other drinks, bananas, raisins, salad and pizza to everyone.

As the event wound down, clean-up began and vendors began packing up. Under the gazebo area were the food stations. Thirty boxes of pizza had been ordered, and only three remained unopened. I asked one of the staff about taking one of the unopened pizzas...and then related a story of a previous experience of giving away a box of pizza.

A few years before, I had worked at an event all day. The employer ordered many pizzas for our dinner, and one was left unopened. I asked the man who provided the pizzas about taking the one remaining, and giving it to someone. He said, "*Yes, because if you don't take it, I'll just throw it away.*" After work, it was dark, and I drove with the pizza on my passenger front seat. Not knowing who was to receive the pizza, I asked God where to go. My path took me into our lower downtown on a main street with few vehicles on it. On a corner, I spotted a lady pushing a baby stroller with a man walking beside her. I stopped my car and rolled down my window and said, "*Would you like an unopened box of pizza?*" The lady replied, "*This is my brother. He and I just prayed and asked God about providing us with dinner. Now you're here – thanks for the pizza."*

The staff person for the running event appreciated my previous experience with the pizza. She then said, *"Go ahead and take it…and I'd like to know the story about who receives this pizza."* Two men with a church group were nearby. They were building a stage for an event occurring the next day in the park. I told both about my previous pizza story and the older one said, *"Come tomorrow for our church event here and tell us your testimony about giving away this pizza!"* In walking to my car, I marveled about the future destination of the pizza!

As with the delivery a few years earlier, it was dark, too. Before leaving the park, I asked God to direct my path. His answers were not clear, so I proceeded to lower downtown and onto the same street as before. Again, there were few vehicles out and road construction had some of the streets blocked off. I turned onto another street that's the address for a non-profit organization, Springs Rescue Mission. They serve many of our homeless population and others with alcohol and drug addictions. Before I got to their multi-building complex, I spotted a disheveled man sitting on a sidewalk in front of another building. I drove further to the mission's complex, but it was closed and no one was milling around in their parking lot.

I then turned my car around and went back to see the scruffy-looking man on the sidewalk. As I parked my car next to the building a few feet from his sidewalk home, he said, *"Hello."* I handed him the pizza box and he thanked me, while his dog quietly looked at both of us. The man was short in stature and had scraggly brown hair with a full beard. His toenails were calcified and curled. Wanting not to stand over him, I asked if I could sit on his sidewalk. He agreed and I told him about being at a party and my want to save the unopened pizza box for someone else. He told me some of his history – his name was Rick…he hailed from Tyler, Texas…he'd been in Colorado Springs for two years…his age was 71. His temporary home address was the corner part of the sidewalk with his backpack and other belongings spread out. A middle-aged lady was sitting 10 feet away on a driveway curb with her back to us. Rick offered her some of his pizza and she only moaned with a negative response with her hands. Another man slept under a too-short blanket on the sidewalk about 15 feet from Rick's home. He told me he would offer the man some pizza later, after he woke up.

I then asked Rick if I could pray with him. He responded with. *"Yes, and I believe in God and am a Christian."* We prayed with my right hand on his shoulder while I held his hand. Our prayer to God was for Him to give Rick safe travel back to Texas, a miracle for a permanent home and answers to solve his health issues. After our prayer together, I got up and said goodbye to the man with the sidewalk address.

In reading Mark 10:27 and Jeremiah 32:27, I know true power comes from God! Prayer is the greatest gift I can do for others, especially when problems are so complex and good things seem impossible.

QUESTIONS TO PONDER?

❋　*Do I carry the onus of trying to do the impossible?*

❋　*When I pray with others, do I point them to the truth of God that He has the answers? Or instead, do they believe that I have the answers?*

❋　*Do you believe in miracles? Where do they come from?*

❋　*When you give, is it anonymously or is it with fanfare to gain recognition or favor?*

❋　*Do you have ideas to help your community solve or be involved with the homeless issues? Are people who beg for money on street corners really homeless or just panhandlers too lazy to work? How do you determine who to give your time, talents and treasure to?*

34

 My Notes:

_____
_____
_____
_____
_____
_____
_____
_____
_____
_____
_____
_____
_____
_____
_____
_____
_____
_____

LIFE IS FULL OF CHOICES

*A son remembers his father as tough, scrappy, entrepreneurial and one
of the best World War II soldiers of our greatest generation.*

My friend, John Riesberg, brought me two World War II
German weapons that he wanted me to write a story about. One
was a World War II German dagger that was recently shipped to him
from a relative. The dagger was purloined by his father, Sergeant
John Charles Riesberg, when the war ended. The other weapon
was a German bayonet that John purchased at a local flea market.
Because the dagger had a personal connection from John's father to
him, I chose to write the story only about it. *We met at a Panera Bread
in Colorado Springs and with coffee, John began to relate to me about his father.*

The dagger stirred John's memories of his parents, growing
up and the only conversation he had with his father about his
involvement in World War II. After the conversation his mother,
Mary, filled in some of the details that his father did not want to
commiserate about.

John's father was born on a farm in the early 1900s in Vanersberg,
Sweden as Karl Hilding Rësberg. Circa 1920 he relocated by ship
to America and changed his name to John Charles Riesberg and
the only English word he knew was, *"Thank you."* His first job and
living quarters were at New York City's Waldorf Hotel as he gave
out towels in the men's restroom wearing a tuxedo. In Vanersberg,
his wage was the equivalent to $0.75/week and on his first night at
the hotel he earned tips of $0.73! Later he moved to Watertown,
New York and worked retail with the FW Woolworth Co. With an
entrepreneurial spirit, John Charles Riesberg got bored with retail
and landed a job as a financial closer with Manufacturers Hanover.
He also developed a couple of patents – one was sold to an oil
company for $10,000.

Now a naturalized American citizen, Mr. Riesberg enlisted with
the U.S. Army in his early 40s. His leadership was stellar as he earned
five Bronze Stars – Normandy, Rhineland, North France, Ardennes
and Central Europe. He also earned a Silver Star for North France
and fought at the Battle of the Bulge. Sgt. Riesberg was one of the

soldiers who survived Normandy Beach on D-Day, June 6, 1944. In observing hundreds of fellow soldiers die by the German machine gun-fire, he began to count the seconds between the barrages. The delay was 12 seconds…because the German army did not give out the special gloves needed to handle the too-hot-to-touch machine guns. He told John that he was scared to death with the carnage and his options were, "Stay and die or move forward." Later Sgt. Riesberg's superiors implored him to advance to the Lieutenant rank, but he remained a Sergeant by choice.

Sgt. Riesberg was with the 125th Regiment and learned in combat about the end of the war on May 8, 1945 near Cologne, Germany. Getting ready to go home to America, he gathered some of the German weapons and shipped them to a relative in West Plains, Missouri. The fore-mentioned dagger was taken off a German soldier and has Ulles für Deutschland inscribed on the blade. In English it means, "Germany forever."

"Life is full of choices," is what John's father told him. Our freedom is not free and his father chose to defend it paying a heavy price. A few days before his father died, John Sr. lamented to his wife, *"Do you think God has forgiven me for all those men I killed?"* Mary's loving reply was, *"John, the moment you accepted Christ you were and are forgiven for all your sins."* John Charles Riesberg died with his sins forgiven and lives in eternity with Christ.

Reading I John 1:9 reminds me that we all have the choice to believe in God and His Son, Jesus. The good news is – forgiveness is freely given when we simply confess our sins to Him.

QUESTIONS TO PONDER?

❋ *Do I dwell on the past, present or future?*

❋ *Have I forgiven myself for things I'm not proud of?*

❋ *Do I need to ask God and others for forgiveness?*

❋ *Do I believe I've been forsaken?*

My Notes:

_____

_____

_____

_____

_____

_____

_____

_____

_____

_____

_____

_____

_____

_____

_____

_____

_____

WHERE ARE THE INSTRUCTIONS?

In visiting our home, our five-year-old grandnephew
was curious about an old grandfather mantle chime clock
resting on the floor next to my study.

One of our grandnephews, Ridge, age five, came for a visit to our home with his sister, Rainey, age 10. They came in early summer after school was out. Before the trip, Ridge was somewhat apprehensive about staying for *"four sleeps"* and tried to negotiate with my wife and his mother for a shorter stay. He finally decided to come with his sister for the four days and nights; it was Ridge's first visit and one of many for Rainey.

My wife drove to pick them up and right after arriving to our home, the kids chose where they would sleep and unloaded their one suitcase. In showing Ridge around the house, I took him first to my study on the lower level. He looked around and said, *"I like this place...and I really like your office!"* As we walked out of it into the den area, he saw an old grandfather clock resting on the floor next to my study. It's a mantle chime clock that was made by one of my great grandfathers, circa 1850.

Ridge crouched down in front of the dormant clock and looked at it intently. He opened the clock door and began looking at the pieces and asked, *"Where are the instructions?"* I told him, *"There are no instructions."* With that I rued, *"He's going to break the clock,"* but then thought, *"It doesn't work anyway, and it would be a challenge for him."*

A note inside the clock explaining its origin was written by my Aunt Grace about her mother (my grandmother): *"Sarah Edwards Castle (1881-1974) remembers her grandfather, Daniel Shaw Edwards. Her other grandfather, William Knight, lived across the road from the school house. She remembered him winding this clock every night when she was a little girl on their farm near Adrian, Michigan."*

As Ridge was sticking his little hands inside the openings at the top of the clock, he worked the clock mechanism. He looked like he knew what he was doing, so I went back to my study.

Suddenly, I heard the 165-year-old grandfather clock chiming! In walking out to the den, I praised him with, *"That's great Ridge – thanks!"* He was very pleased with his successful effort.

For the rest of his visit, Ridge went downstairs often. Each time, he first stopped at the clock to get it chiming again. On the last night of their stay, Ridge asked us if he could stay for another *"sleep."* Because plans were already made for the kids to go home, we told him that he could simply visit us again.

In reading Matthew 18:2-6, we are blessed to have children in our home. I can learn much from them as they are gifts from God.

QUESTIONS TO PONDER?

❋   *The innocence of children – what they say without provocation, how they view challenges with simplicity and what reality is to them – should make us adults laugh, smile and think. What do you do to encourage the children in your life?*

❋   *If a child was given the opportunity to teach you something, what lesson would it be?*

❋   *When children are guests in your home, business or where you meet them, do you treat them with respect?*

❋   *Who will the children you know emulate and become like?*

❋   *What are great and poor examples of leading children?*

My Notes:

SHIFTING GEARS

*Facing the reality of my depression is really about swallowing my pride,
asking for help and adjusting.*

Several years ago my wife and I dropped our medical
insurance because it became too costly. In our late 50s, our medical
insurance premiums were hundreds of dollars per month even
with the highest deductible available. Our income had dropped
significantly due to a job loss a few years before. With few job
prospects during the Great Recession, we were faced with many
financial challenges, and with no healthcare coverage we were
unprotected physically.

From printed advertising, I learned about a community
healthcare service. With a choice of getting healthcare that used
county dollars and private donations, I swallowed my pride and
we applied for the service. A few weeks later our applications
were accepted.

I have struggled with depression since I was 16. It's a disease,
a chemical imbalance in my brain, and a hereditary condition in
the Castle family. My grandfather was a manic depressive, an uncle
suffered a nervous breakdown at age 18 and my father suffered
with depression, too. In our family we did not talk about the
disease; I believe that perpetuated the stigma even more. When I
was 17, I learned from a family friend how my grandfather died;
he committed suicide on my father's 16th birthday. Mom told me
about Dad taking depression medication, but Dad and I did not
talk about such things.

"Shifting gears" is the expression I have used to describe my ups
and downs with euphoria and depression. I get bored easily and
whenever I began to sink into depression the possibilities became
impossible and I started to dwell on what I could not change.
Then I would shift gears by changing jobs, adding excitement,
going window shopping and occupying my time with activities.

Soon after starting with the healthcare service, I opted to be on depression medication. After a few months, I deduced that I was feeling much better and no longer needed the medication. My reasoning was false and I deceived myself. Without the anti-depressant drug continually improving my chemical imbalance, I lapsed into depression again over time.

Three years passed and I began to feel overwhelmed, frozen even with small details, avoided challenges and wanted to be alone. It was depression again. My wife and a small men's church group recognized the signs. I made an appointment with my doctor and she prescribed some anti-depression medication. Within a few days, my chemical imbalance greatly improved and I felt much better! Not being a medical doctor, I suspect my chemical imbalance gets more pronounced as I get older.

After taking the medication for a couple of weeks, I attended a non-profit's board meeting. Before the program started the director of communications for my health care service, Randy, seated himself next to me. We had not met before and after introductions I expressed my positive experiences with his employer. I told him about my history with depression, the most recent diagnosis, how I was making progress and the positive effects on my attitude, decisions and outlook on life in general. I also told him about my wife's observation of how much better life was with me since I was on the medication. Giving Randy my business card, I said, *"If you ever want a testimony about your healthcare service, give me a call!*

A few weeks later Randy called. After telling me they wanted to do a video in an interview format, he asked what I hoped to accomplish with my testimony. I told Randy, *"Some of my skill-set includes being direct, open and transparent. My hope is that a potential viewer will opt to get help for their depression, too. Educating people about depression is one of the ways to combat its stigma. As a Christian, God commands me to serve others and this is one way I can do that."*

The completed video was posted on the company's website and on YouTube.

Romans 12:2-8 is a good reminder that God grants me humility to be transparent in my faith. With Ephesians 6:12, I learn that Satan uses my weakness of depression against me in spiritual warfare.

QUESTIONS TO PONDER?

✵ *The statistics show that one in four people suffer from some form of depression. How can I be more compassionate in my speech and actions knowing that I may be speaking to someone with depression?*

✵ *With the subject of depression, how can I open a conversation or impart details about my challenges with it?*

My Notes:

THE CHRISTMAS CARD

*Having the Christmas spirit all year round gives me the opportunity
to give to others and encourage people. It has been a blessing!*

When I learned that a faraway friend was quite depressed, I
gave him a call. As we talked, I began to realize that David had
the frightening tone of suicide in his voice and we talked for a
couple of hours.

After the call, I thought, *"What more can I do for my friend?"*
Then I saw the framed cartoon on my desk. It was a copy of a
1939 advertisement that had been given to me 15 years earlier. I
removed the cartoon from the frame and faxed it to my friend's
office. A few days later I called him back and he said, *"Where'd you
get that corny cartoon? I haven't laughed this hard in years!"* We laughed
together. David was much more upbeat than in our previous call.

A simple cartoon and giving my friend something to smile
and laugh about made such an impact! After that, I made 200
copies of the cartoon entitled "Joe's TEMPER Almost BROKE
UP Their HOME." I also added the ditty: "May this 1939 cartoon
give you grins. Laugh and then share it with friends. Merry
Christmas, Happy Holidays and a great New Year to you, your
friends and family for a lot of cheer! Come visit us in Colorado
Springs, Colorado!" I'm not sure how many of the cartoons I've
given (it's probably over 2,500), but it has become my impromptu
Christmas card. In fact, I keep them in my car to give away to
people I meet and to friends I see all year round.

Here are a few of the most memorable moments these
Christmas cards have brought:

- I stopped at the only grocery store in Corrigan, Texas on
  an early Sunday morning before Christmas on my way to
  see my parents in Nacogdoches. I took three Christmas
  cards with me. I gave the first two to grocery store clerks,
  but the third one was not as easy to give away. I found

myself in the grocery store's coffee-sitting area with another man. He was in a wheelchair and was quite gruff in appearance and demeanor. I gave him the card and said, *"Merry Christmas,"* but he refused to take it. He probably thought I was trying to sell him something. So I tried again and said something like, *"It's simply a Christmas card and I wanted you to have one."* He did not take the card again so I said, *"This is my gift to you, Merry Christmas!"* He took the Christmas card and as I was walking away the man said in a very low voice, *"Merry Christmas."*

- When I worked for a regional Chamber of Commerce in Houston, I had the privilege of getting to know the Chairman of the Board and his long-time assistant, Mary. Their jobs for the chamber were voluntary, so her duties included planning many of the chamber functions. She was very quiet and didn't say much. Generally, my interaction with her was brief. Right before the Chamber's Christmas party, I gave Mary one of the Christmas cards. She looked at it with no expression as I left their office. The next day, I went to the party and saw her at the main table. She said, *"Mr. Castle, I've given away 10 copies of the cartoon. Thank you and Merry Christmas!"*

- I enjoy Blizzards from Dairy Queen. I made a stop at a Dairy Queen and as I was getting out of my car I saw a metro bus driver leaving his bus for a break. As he was headed into the store I said, *"Would you like a Christmas card?"* His response was, *"Gee, I never get Christmas cards and I'm getting one from a complete stranger!"*

As corny as the Christmas cards are, it's been a joy giving them away. My only agenda has been to help someone smile or laugh.

John 3:16 and Psalm 46:1 remind me
that I serve as God's messenger.
The Lord gives hope, refuge, love, mercy, grace
and eternity for those who believe in Him.

QUESTIONS TO PONDER?

❋   *What is my agenda, motivation or purpose
     when I communicate, present or sell?*

❋   *Am I pleasant to be around…and when I
     leave a conversation, are people smiling, appreciative
     and thankful for our time together?*

❋ *What signs (body language, tone of voice, facial expressions,
     and apparel neatness) indicate my intent before I speak?*

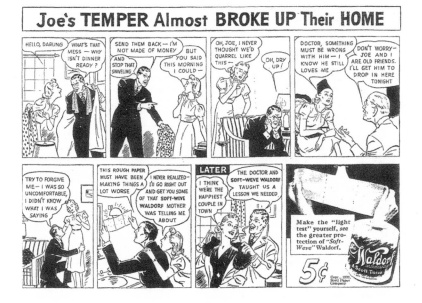

Used with Permission by ©Kimberly-Clark Worldwide, Inc.

My Notes:

EXPECT THE MOST!

In learning about the challenges of a young lady working behind a sandwich shop counter, I decided to let God influence my decisions to make some positive differences in her life.

I frequented a local sandwich shop for lunch in Colorado Springs. Each time I order a meal, I am treated well and enjoy conversation with the other patrons and employees. Even though I'm more comfortable in being called *Charles*, the manager and his staff always call me *Mr. Castle*.

One of the employees, Sarah, was always energetic, smiles and treats me well each time I patronize the shop. After she'd been working there for four months – I knew little about her. One late afternoon, when Sarah and I were the only people there, I asked her to review an editorial I was drafting about homelessness for a local print publication. In scanning the 250-word document, she suggested two points for clarification, and I immediately edited them into my editorial. Later, as she was doing some sweeping and mopping work in the seating area, she said to me, *"I don't think you know this Mr. Castle – I'm homeless."*

I asked, *"Are you living in your car?"* and she replied, *"No, I'm couch-surfing at a friend's home with my two children.* Sarah then told me her three-old son and two-year daughter were in a daycare center a block away from the sandwich shop. She also said that transportation for them was our local bus service, since she did not own or have access to a car.

I usually don't carry much cash on me, but that day was different as I had $114 on me. I got a nudge from God to give her all my cash! I resisted and reasoned for about 10 seconds, that my need was greater than His nudge and Sarah's need. My words flowed with, *"Then this is for you,"* as I gave her the five $20s in my wallet! Sarah began to cry and we prayed for God's blessing to be upon her. Later, after her shift was done, I walked with Sarah to the day care center as she picked up her children. She said, *"My faith is the only thing that I hang onto every day. I pray daily and God delivers us with His provision."* There was another $14 in my pocket, left over from my lunch order, and I gave her that money then, too.

About six weeks later, Sarah told me a man in her church was helping her get an apartment. She said, *"I'm using all that money you gave me for the deposit on the apartment!"* Later, some friends helped her move into her new home. A few weeks later, she told me her children were adapting well since the stress of constant moving was gone.

One afternoon, I asked her how she was doing. Sarah said she had paid bills the day before and broke even…and lamented that she needed to earn more money so they could get ahead. A few days later, the subject of birthdays came up and I asked, *"Mine's in March, when's yours?"* Sarah said, *"My 24th birthday is two weeks from this Friday."* God nudged me again with, *"Tell her to expect the most for her birthday."* For the next two weeks, as I went through the sandwich shop line each time, I said to Sarah, *"Expect the most for your birthday."*

Sunday afternoons during the NFL football season is at-home time for my wife and me. On the Sunday before Sarah's birthday, I envisioned how to make her birthday a special one. I crafted an email and sent it individually to many friends in Colorado Springs. It partially read, *"Sarah is a friend who works at a sandwich shop at (location). Her 24th birthday is this coming Friday. Until recently, she was homeless and couch-surfing at friends' homes. A church member recently helped her get a home, she relies on bus transportation and does not own a car. Sarah is a single-mother with a three-year-old son and a two-year-old daughter and when I asked her what she wanted for her birthday she said, 'I want…no, I need bus passes.'*

I purchased a birthday card for Sarah and will take it by with some cash in it. I'll deliver it personally to her this week at her work location. Will you take by a birthday card to her this week? And pass this email to others – it would wonderful if she received many birthday cards, good wishes and prayers!

The things of God will continue to perplex, amaze and confound me until the day I die. For me, and perhaps you, serving Sarah is being the hands and feet of Christ. God bless you, Charles."

One of my friends that received the email decided to put

my request into our weekly church men's group newsletter. Two days later at our Tuesday morning coffee, Man Moment and Bible teaching, I laid out some birthday cards for the men to select. As men came in the door – many put cash in a community card or selected a personal one. As we were wrapping up our men's group, some of the cards were left on the table. I then approached men to take a card to send to their wives or someone else they loved, mail it – so their loved one *"got mail."* One man wrote a letter to his wife right then, thought it was a great idea and told me he'd rarely written his wife at all in their 11 years of marriage.

After leaving our men's group, I took the community card and the others into the sandwich shop where Sarah worked. The manager said, *"Sarah is not here today because she needed a day off to do some important personal things. And she's never asked for a day off before, so I gave it to her."* I then went to our downtown main bus terminal to find out about purchasing bus passes. When I got there, I learned the bus-pass machine was broken so I located the on-site manager. She explained the machine had been broken for weeks and where I could buy bus passes at other locations. Then to my left, Sarah walked up to me. She had been to her important appointment earlier that morning and was on the way to her next stop. I was quite surprised to bump into Sarah so I went to retrieve her birthday cards from my car. In giving them to her, Sarah said, *"Mr. Castle, I couldn't tell you this before…Brian, (the manager at the sandwich shop), gave me a raise and is training me to become a manager!"* I then gave her a hug and shouted, *"Praise God!"* We then prayed amongst the people in the bus terminal.

I believe Sarah received lots of birthday cards with cash, bus passes and notes from many she did not know. Besides saving most of the money, she told me the gifts were used for buying more bus passes and two long-sleeved shirts for herself, taking her children out to dinner and paying down a personal debt.

Sarah told me recently she opened her home to a homeless mother trying to get custody of her child again. She told her, *"Save your money for an apartment and stay on my couch."* The woman is now looking for a job, getting back on her feet because of Sarah's compassion and is revisiting her Christian faith.

In reading I John 2:3-6,
I wonder what my actions say about my Christian belief.

QUESTIONS TO PONDER?

✸   *Do I do walk the walk or only talk the talk*
in proclaiming Jesus as my Savior?

✸   *How do I determine what is a nudge from God?*

✸   *Every person has a story and wants to be*
loved, so why should I listen to them?

✸   *When I don't have the resources, time, talents*
and money – who do I choose to help?

✸   *Do I measure up in being the hands and feet of*
Christ? I wonder who is watching what I do.

My Notes:

_____

_____

_____

_____

_____

_____

_____

_____

_____

_____

_____

_____

_____

_____

_____

_____

_____

SHE ONLY ASKED FOR PRAYER

Filling-in-the-blanks for a young single mother was an honor.
I watched her Christian faith in action as she prayed, requested prayer
and depended on God for the results. Another short story,
Expect the Most!, is also about this young lady, Sarah.

I met Sarah in the sandwich shop where she worked. In frequenting the store a couple of times a week, I got to know her smile, genuine positive attitude, strong faith and plights. When I first met Sarah, she was homeless and surfing on friends' couches, using our Colorado Springs' bus system and taking care of her three-year-old son and two-year-old daughter. Because of family abuse, she kept her personal information private.

Knowing of the abuse, I honored her quest for privacy. In the beginning, the only contact information I knew was her first name and where she worked. Each time I saw Sarah at the sandwich shop, I asked how she was doing and listened for needs I could pray for. Her church was her biggest mainstay and members helped her get an apartment. I organized our church men's group to give her a special 24th birthday with cards, gifts and cash. Only six weeks before she left Colorado Springs, Sarah gave me her last name, address, email and phone number.

Sarah was ecstatic when her ex-husband became a Christian and was baptized at her church. She wanted her family back together – and after his baptism – Sarah began to talk about their plans for the future. She had three goals – take herself, her ex-husband and children to a far-away city with a warmer climate; get a college education; and open a restaurant business in the near future. To most people – Sarah's dreams probably seemed impossible, hopeless and very far-fetched. For me – Sarah had the ambition, zing and faith to get anything done!

One of my friends, Robert, told me that he and his wife, Sharon, were moving back to Denver. The couple has been married for 53 years and Robert said, *"We planned to sell our 17-year-old car, but God told us we would give it away…and He would bring us the recipient."*

Robert had been coming to our church men's group for 1-1/2 years and I had been in small-group gatherings with him. He said, *"When Sharon and I thought about selling our 1999 Mazda, God said, "No, you're not; you'll give it away and I'll bring the person to you whom you'll give it to.""* About two weeks after Robert's conversation with God, I called him about their car. I said, *"Robert, have you given your car away yet?"* He said, *"No."* I then asked, *"Would you consider giving it to Sarah, whom I wrote the 'Expect the Most!' story about?"* Robert said, *"Yes... and it's done."* We made arrangements to transfer the title to Sarah a couple of days later and meet to give her the car in 1-1/2 weeks.

I made arrangements to take Sarah to Robert and Sharon's home so she could pick up her new car. I picked her up in front of her home...and felt a little odd. This was the first time Sarah was in my presence, and not serving me. I began to talk to Sarah like a daughter, as we went to Robert and Sharon's home to pick up her 'new' car! Sarah then made a comment to me that will resonate with me the rest of my life, *"Mr. Castle, this is the first time I've ever received anything without conditions!"* I almost drove into a snowbank! At age 24, Sarah, was telling me something that was quite foreign to me. I then asked her to consider telling Robert and Sharon what she told me when we met them a few minutes later.

Sarah and I arrived at Robert and Sharon's home 15 minutes later. We rang the doorbell, were received with open arms and walked into their living room. I asked Robert, Sharon and Sarah about praying together. Sarah then told Robert and Sharon what she had told me in the car about receiving her first gift without conditions. Sharon then said, *"Then we know this car is for you!"*

Leaving the three of them, I made an excuse to go outside and start brushing off the snow from the car. Sharon and Sarah exchanged contact info so they could keep in touch. The car had 18 inches of snow on it from our previous snow storm...so I began prepping the car for its new owner. Sarah came outside shortly afterwards, saw our progress and helped coordinate the glove box info and trunk contents. Soon afterwards, Sarah followed me in her new car to a local Panera Bread restaurant.

I said that lunch was my treat...and she ordered the least on the menu. As we sat at a table, I understood that the lady in front of me, Sarah, was put in my path by God. I said, *"If I had a daughter, I'd want her to be just like you!"* She was having three "new" used tires installed on her car to make it safer. When we met at a local Wal-Mart later to exchange the old license plates, Sarah's children hugged me and her ex-husband shook my hand.

Not hearing from Sarah for a few weeks, I assumed she was leaving Colorado Springs soon. Then I got a text from Sarah... asking for prayer. With her children, she was being followed by her mother's boyfriend to find out where she was going. That same day, Sarah, was planning to drive from her leased apartment to her new home state in Miami, Florida. Sarah's mother, who initiated the family abuse and wanted to enforce control over Sarah, had stalled her trip by calling county authorities. Now, with some legal complications, Sarah's trip was delayed and she had no place to stay or go. I texted her back and asked her to meet me at a local motel in 45 minutes. I actually followed her car into the motel at the same time as she drove in. It took some time, but Sarah was able to lose her mother's boyfriend by driving into the parking lot of a local police sub-station.

I paid for Sarah and her children's first night at the motel. In wondering how I could afford or manage Sarah's continuing plight, I prayed to God for answers. That night, I sent out an email to the church men's group and others for answers for ideas on Sarah and her children's impending condition. Soon afterwards, I received an email from one of the men, Bruce, about meeting Sarah, her children and me the next morning at the motel. Bruce's wife's mother had just died a few hours before and he wanted to give toward Sarah's hope. He took the four of us out to breakfast and then paid for one week of Sarah and her children's stay at the motel. This gave her time to fetter out all the problems and to figure out what to do next.

I got a text from Sarah about a week later that the holdups had been solved and all four – her ex-husband, the kids and her – were leaving town on Tuesday morning. From the men's group, I gathered notes, cash and met Sarah in the motel parking lot the next morning. I prayed with Sarah and her ex-, and I believe her future husband again, in the parking lot.

My job for Sarah was to pray for her plight, ask God to intervene and for me not to judge her past, present and choices she makes for the future. An interesting point – the only thing Sarah ever asked me for was prayer.

*Reading Matthew 7:1-5 and Luke 6:38 give me hope that
I am not the answer to all the problems of the world.*

QUESTIONS TO PONDER?

❉　*Do I believe that the greatest gift I
can give to someone is prayer?*

❉　*What does the birth and resurrection of this Jesus mean to me?*

❉　*What kind of impact can I make on one person
— in gifts, prayers and communications?*

❉　*When I see and feel evil — what do I
do to get beyond and around it?*

❉　*Do I recognize evil when I see it? And where
did it come from — Satan, me or others?*

❉　*For the next time I see Sarah, what should
I say and do for her and her family?*

My Notes:

_____

_____

_____

_____

_____

_____

_____

_____

_____

_____

_____

_____

_____

_____

_____

_____

_____

_____

_____

_____

THE HOMELESS MAN

*Being the same person to everyone – open, transparent and not hypocritical –
is much easier said than done.*

One afternoon, I was moping around the house because I had just received some disturbing news. My wife said, *"Why don't you go out and give yourself away!"* So, instead of feeling sorry for myself, I did as she suggested and looked for someone to serve.

I drove south of downtown Colorado Springs to an area with many run-down and older homes. Then I spotted some trees in esplanades on one of our avenues that needed trimming. Sadly, our city had suffered its worst cutback ever in funding maintenance for city land, parks and recreation. No one had trimmed these trees—which went on for about four blocks—for quite some time. In fact, many of the saplings had grown into mini-trees. I decided to help out. It felt good to do some manual labor and it took my mind off of my fretting.

Then, I saw a man sitting in the grass in the middle of the four blocks. When I finished trimming all the trees, the man was still sitting in the grass. With his backpack next to him he appeared to be homeless. I started a conversation with the man and I asked if he had read the same book I was reading at the time. We made other small talk, and I asked if I could sit in the grass with him. He said, *"Yes."*

He told me his name was Red. And he began to unravel his story of being a restaurant chef in town, losing his job, and having a fallout with his family. He was even evicted from his home and lost his belongings. In a short time he had no income, no job and no place to live. Red was now homeless.

I asked if he had eaten recently. Red said he had eaten and our conversation steered towards the restaurant industry, books we both had read and other topics. I asked him again if he was hungry and he said, *"No."* Then Red said he had to go because the shelter where he was staying opened every afternoon at 4:30. Red and I were sitting three blocks from his temporary new home, the

Salvation Army.

I asked him, *"Can I pray with you?"*

Red said, *"Yes,"* and he told me of his Christian faith. Then we prayed together.

Red got ready to leave, and as he crossed the street he said to me, *"You acknowledged me, talked with me, asked me twice if I had eaten and then prayed with me. You're different than most people. Thanks for stopping to see me."*

After he'd gone, I continued with the tree trimming, and as I remembered our conversation and Red's parting words, I felt blessed. In serving a homeless man, God blessed me.

When I read Luke 11:5-10, I ask,
what kind of messenger am I for God?
Do my actions match and measure up to my
Christian faith and belief in Christ?

QUESTIONS TO PONDER?

❋   *Why do bad things happen to good people?*

❋   *Why do good things happen to bad people?*

❋   *What are my principles and foundations for guideposts that determine who are good and bad people?*

❋   *When does it even out?*

My Notes:

WHERE'D YOU COME FROM?

Watching a lady fish through her credit cards and listening to her questions to a deli shop manager, I believed she was hungry and looking for the cheapest thing on their menu.

Often during the work week, I eat lunch at several locations of a popular deli chain's restaurants around Colorado Springs. After a morning of appointments and doing some cold-calling, I stopped for lunch at one of the deli shops south of downtown. I got the day special and sat down to eat.

Toward the end of my meal, I noticed a nicely-dressed woman come into the restaurant. She plopped down her large purse onto one of the unoccupied tables and located her wallet. Spread across both of her hands were many credit cards; after a few minutes of silent discord she chose one of them. The woman was the only person in line and began asking the manager behind the counter about prices on the placard menu. Her questions centered on the cheapest food items.

God prompts me to do things that usually cost me money, sacrifice my time, popularity and convenience or to give away talents. In observing the actions of the woman in the deli shop, the Lord prompted me to give her some money. I looked in my wallet, only to find two one-dollar bills. Then, I went out to my car and opened the console where I kept some extra cash. I pulled out a $20 bill and walked back into the restaurant.

As I approached the lady patron, she was still the only person in line and no one else was in the restaurant. I gently walked up to her with the twenty and said, *"This is for you."* As I put my hand on her shoulder, she looked at me with surprise. She then replied, *"Where'd you come from?"* Her eyes welled up with tears, and I told her I was just a regular person who came into the store on occasion. Then, I left the restaurant to resume working.

The next day, I was in lower downtown for lunchtime and went to the same deli shop. After ordering a sandwich meal, I pulled out my wallet to pay. Then, the server behind the counter asked, *"Aren't you the man that gave the money to the lady yesterday?"* I said, *"Yes."* He said, *"The manager from yesterday told the rest of us what you did. She was inspired by your action and it restored her faith in people. Today, I'm giving you a discount off your sandwich."*

In reading Proverbs 19:17 and Hebrews 13:16, I'm blessed to have a close relationship with God!

QUESTIONS TO PONDER?

✳ *What does sacrificial giving mean to you?*

✳ *What do you think of the comment, "If it's good, it comes from God; if it's selfish, it comes from me."?*

✳ *Do you pray for discernment when asked to give your time, talents or treasure?*

✳ *What does privacy and anonymity mean to you when it comes to giving?*

✳ *Are you humble and pious when you give?*

My Notes:

_____

_____

_____

_____

_____

_____

_____

_____

_____

_____

_____

_____

_____

_____

_____

_____

_____

_____

YOU CAN PRAY FOR ME

In affirming a Church official in his stand on a controversial world issue,
I came to know what really mattered to him.

After visiting a friend in one of our Colorado Springs hospitals, I took the elevator down to the foyer on the first floor. Going into a quiet lounge area near the front door, I found a newspaper to read and sat down in a comfortable chair.

In the publication, I spotted an article written by a prominent local Church official. It was his monthly column. In this writing, he wrote that periodically people who attend their denomination of churches approach him for an appointment.

Sometimes, the subject matter is to discuss the tenets of faith of the Church. At some point in the meeting, the guests suggest that he and the Church should change their tenets of faith to include their beliefs. Often, because the visitors don't get their way, they become agitated and angry. They then stomp out of his office saying a number of expletives that are not very kind.

After I finished reading the official's article, God asked me to affirm him in his stand on the Christian principle. I then drove a couple of miles south from the hospital to his office. In the building's parking lot, I wrote a postcard to the official including these notes: *"You and I are both Christians. People who do not truly believe that our faith is based on what God says in His Bible are misled. Most of them do not have the hope for eternal life, and believe life on earth, is the best it will ever be. You and I know – here on earth is the worst it will ever be. This is why they want to change our faith to conform to their ways, not God's."*

About a month later, I received a note card from the Church official. He said, *"Thank you for your kind words and affirming me in my stand."* Afterwards, from time to time, I would drop by his office and leave a note or calendar, thanking him for his service to God. Right before Thanksgiving, 18 months after receiving his thank-you card, I asked his secretary for a face-to-face appointment with him in his office. Our meeting lasted about 30 minutes and then we prayed. I then asked, *"What can I do for you?"* He looked directly at me and quietly breathed, *"You can pray for me."*

As I left his office, I knew I'd been in the presence of a humble man who knew he was just as fallible as me. Some may think that his position of power in the Church, makes him above the rest of us. But, to be accountable to God and men, he needs our prayers, too.

I am thankful that this leader in the Church follows God's Word and does not change his Christian beliefs to satisfy others. From knowing this man, I believe he prays for those who dislike and or sin against him.

In reading I Timothy 2:1-4, I believe God is pleased when we pray for our leaders, whether we like their decisions or not.

QUESTIONS TO PONDER?

✳ *Whether I like the leadership that is elected, appointed or given (parent, guardian or friend) to me... who are some of them that I can pray for?*

✳ *We have seen some leaders fall flat on their faces. I wonder how many of them were alone, had no one or few to confide in or even ask us to pray for them. How can you communicate with leaders in your community and let them know you are praying for them?*

✳ *Accountability is about being transparent with difficult issues, past sins and walking in wisdom to make better future choices. Who do I trust to meet with once or regularly to develop accountability?*

✳ *What's God got to do with accountability?*

✳ *What does the Bible mean to you and do you seek the wisdom in it?*

My Notes:

_____

_____

_____

_____

_____

_____

_____

_____

_____

_____

_____

_____

_____

_____

_____

_____

_____

_____

DEAR DAD

My father said some harsh words to my wife while she was visiting my parents. When my wife returned home, she told me about the confrontation and how hurt she felt. I pondered my words and six weeks later mailed him this letter.

Dear Dad,   7/1/83

These are some of the things that I remember you and I have done together:

When Mom was having her back surgery and you were sitting at the kitchen bar at the home in Dallas. I didn't understand the seriousness of her operation; you said she could die if the surgeon made a wrong cut. I was late for school that day.

When you and I went kite flying on the interstate before it opened up in Beaumont at Calder & I-10.

When you bailed me out of jail in University Park.

When you gave me advice and wrote a letter concerning Stone's Garage in Nacogdoches when I was just two weeks into college.

When you were spraying bug spray on your plants in Houston and I was thinking of inviting Cindy for lunch. She was newly divorced from her husband, and you said it could be a bad situation from his hot temper.

Smoking cigars.

Driving with you and Mom from Houston to Monument Hill just before Sherm's & my wedding.

Having lunch with you at the Hyatt Regency in downtown Houston and on the way back to your office discussing the Bakke *reverse discrimination* case.

Visiting you at the Medical Arts Building in Dallas when you had those laser beam eye operations.

Waking me up in the mornings in your pajama bottoms and slippers. *"Rous minum, Charles!"*

Waiting for you at the American Bank Building in Beaumont or was it the railway station?

These are memories that have come to mind as I'm sitting here today.

Love Charles

Five years later, Dad and I were talking about things and the subject of this letter came up. He said, "What was that letter about...I didn't understand why you sent it?" I then told him how much his words had hurt Sherma, and I did not know what to do or say. The only thing I knew to do was to express my love for him. Dad felt horrible and we talked how time had healed the wounds.

After my father died, I found the letter in the top dresser drawer with his socks and underwear. Mom said he always treasured it and that he felt much loved by my words.

In reading I Corinthians 16:13 and Matthew 6:14-15,
I relied on God's wisdom on how to forgive my father.

QUESTIONS TO PONDER?

❋ *Is it easier to forgive those I know and love or those who are only acquaintances?*

❋ *What are some other ways to forgive people besides asking them in person?*

❋ *Who could I send a note, postcard, email or call today to mend fences, repair a relationship or open doors to communications?*

My Notes:

_____

_____

_____

_____

_____

_____

_____

_____

_____

_____

_____

_____

_____

_____

_____

_____

_____

_____

NO BITTERNESS IN YOUR HEART

In a difficult situation, God showed me that praying for an organization and its members was better than becoming bitter towards them.

At one time, I was part of a Christian men's organization in Houston and Colorado Springs. It was a mainstay of Bible studies, seminars, monthly luncheons and retreats that helped me learn more about my faith, connect with business people and make close friendships.

After being with the organization for eight years in Colorado Springs, I was asked to attend an appointment with its leader. I did not know the subject matter and met him at his office. To my surprise, he informed me I could no longer participate with the organization unless I did what he and the leadership demanded. Their requirements included: I change jobs; they said I was disobeying one of God's commandments; and that I needed to seek a diagnosis for a medical condition. And, if I did not do what they demanded, then I was no longer welcome in the organization.

The leader and his team did not participate in my income earning or medical program. And, they falsely accused me of a sin based on hearsay. I told the leader to immediately take my name off all of their communications.

A few days later, the leader wanted to clarify what he communicated in the first meeting, so we met again. For that meeting, I asked a friend to be present to listen with a second set of ears. The only difference between the first and second meeting, was I could still participate with the organization, but not be in any leadership position. *"No, thanks,"* was my reply as I had said a week earlier.

God has a funny sense of humor! In my sales work and volunteering, I encountered many of the organization's men all over the city. Some would ask me, *"Why haven't you been to the Bible studies, luncheons or seminars lately?"* I would tell them the truth in love and sometimes my answers got back to the leadership. The leader sent me angry emails which told me where his heart was with God. I also encountered men who had been ostracized by the organization.

Some of these men's situations involved divorce, suicide and opposing theological opinions with the leadership's position.

I was angry with the leadership for their actions. But I knew my anger would turn to bitterness if not curbed by God. After a few weeks of brooding, God reminded me of The Parable of Jesus Christ about the Good Samaritan. He tempered my heart with, *"I know you're feeling like the traveler now in the Good Samaritan story, but you can't stay there for long. I want you to think about who you want to feel and be like – the priest, the Levite or the Good Samaritan?"* I read the Good Samaritan parable in Luke 10:30-37 and began to pray for the organization. My anger subsided and my heartfelt pity for the organization and the men in it.

A few days later, I met with my friend Randy, who was one of the organization's key leaders but not privy to their recent decision. He wanted to learn what had happened and make sense of it. After I related my account to him he said, *"Charles, I see no bitterness in your heart."*

As I read Galatians 1:10, I believe God was
showing me to seek His glory.
Though I do not understand why things happen,
I believe God is sovereign.
I am thankful for Him tempering my heart
with His grace, mercy and love by showing me
to be like the Good Samaritan!

QUESTIONS TO PONDER?

❋   *Do I have the discernment to see when my anger is turning into bitterness?*

❋   *Am I a leader for my family, work and organizations that I'm associated with?*

❋   *What are my best communication methods… and do they work as well as I think they do?*

My Notes:

_____

_____

_____

_____

_____

_____

_____

_____

_____

_____

_____

_____

_____

_____

_____

_____

_____

_____

PRESBYTERIAN GENTLEMAN

*In fleeting moments, I will make a gesture that reminds me
of my father or will look in the mirror and see a likeness of him.*

The Christmas after my father died was especially difficult
for our family. Mom missed Dad terribly, as she still lived in their
home with all the memories. A few weeks before Christmas she
received a letter from one of Dad's law colleagues. The letter to
her read as:

> I have thought of you often and intended to write
> sooner, but now is the time. I just wanted to let you know
> that Howard was a very special friend to me. Not only
> did he give me a chance when I was a very green, young
> lawyer, but he took me under his wing and taught me how
> international business is conducted. He was a trailblazer
> for (the company) in those early years, traveling to
> Europe, Russia and China to negotiate extremely large,
> complex transactions. He always came back with fantastic
> stories about places that seemed very exotic to me. I also
> enjoyed his somewhat bawdy limericks, which he loved to
> pass along to all of the young women at (the company),
> just to see if he could get a reaction. I know he was a
> very righteous Presbyterian gentleman, and I suppose his
> poetry was just another side to a very well rounded man.
> I always thought it was pretty amusing.
>
> I think of Howard when I pick roses from my garden.
> He was the one who got me started in the rose growing
> adventure, and although I never was as much of a rose
> devotee as he was, I have always loved them. I will never
> forget how he brought roses to all of the women in the
> office, especially in the early spring when the weather was
> still cool and the summer heat had not yet started wilting

the flowers. I know you miss Howard very much, but surely you know that you shared a full, rich life with a very unique individual who never failed to give to those around him. I hope this Christmas finds you healthy and happy, enjoying the season with friends and family.

A copy of the letter is framed in my study and I read it often.

In reading Proverbs 22:6 and II Timothy 3:14-17,
I was blessed by my parents who loved me dearly.

QUESTIONS TO PONDER?

❋   *For those deceased and still alive, what are three things*
you best remember about your father, mother and others?

❋   *To a stranger on a downtown corner in Houston, I said,*
"Nice tie!" The man replied, "Wow, I haven't gotten a compliment
in months – thanks." Who can I offer a compliment to?

❋   *When I pass from this world to heaven*
– what will people write about me?

My Notes:

_____

_____

_____

_____

_____

_____

_____

_____

_____

_____

_____

_____

_____

_____

_____

_____

_____

_____

BY YOUR SIDE

The gift of life is very precious. God gave me the opportunity to candidly and gently tell my father some positive things before his heart surgery.

My father was physically fit, 5'7" at his tallest height and swimming was his exercise of choice. His broad shoulders and bronze tan made me look like an Albino in comparison. Into his early 80s, Dad swam 650 breast strokes a day against the water jets in their outside home spa.

One day, my father made an appointment with his doctor with the lament, *"For some reason I now only have the stamina to do 250 breast strokes instead of the 650 I was doing a few weeks ago."* His doctor was stunned by the 250 number per day, let alone the 650! The doctor scheduled an appointment with a local cardiologist for an arteriogram a few days later. My mother and I were there for the arteriogram and Dad's aorta had ballooned to four inches wide. With internal bleeding, it was leaking blood at the valve. The cardiologist said it was a miracle it had not ruptured and strongly urged my father to get a second doctor's opinion.

Dad's next doctor's appointment was almost two weeks later in a Houston hospital renowned for their heart medical prowess. When the Houston heart specialist viewed the arteriogram, he said the only option was heart surgery and it had to be done immediately. My father balked and wanted to go home and think about it. Only with strong persistence did the doctor convince him to have the surgery right away, so it was scheduled for the next morning.

Right after his appointment, Dad was checked into a hospital room. My father viewed many things through a pessimist lens and told me he thought he wouldn't survive the surgery. I was irritated by Dad's negativity and felt his attitude was critical to his survival.

That afternoon I went home and found some pictures of his favorite place in the world. The pictures were of the summer cabin on the Chain 'O Lakes at Waupaca, Wisconsin, where he learned to swim. The next morning, I arrived with the pictures and learned his surgery was delayed for four hours. The extra time with Dad was very special for me and I think for him, too. As I showed him the cabin and lake pictures I asked Dad the rhetorical question, "Do you want to go to Waupaca again?"

His answer was, "Of course, Charles!"

I said, "Dad, if you go into the surgery thinking you're going to die, then I think God takes your viewpoint into consideration. If you go into the surgery asking God to give you more time, then I think He considers that, too. God has the ultimate decision of whether you live or die during the surgery. Will you consider these things before your heart surgery?"

Dad's surgery started in the afternoon and lasted six hours. Not only did he survive the surgery, he lived another two and a half years. Dad and Mom together visited the summer cabin two more times to see family, swim, canoe and enjoy the place he so dearly loved.

Matthew 17:20 increases my faith and
remindsds me that God can do the impossible.
I am thankful the Lord gave us "bonus time" with Dad—a true gift of life.

QUESTIONS TO PONDER?

✳ *In love, how do I respond to others' negative*
comments and general outlook?

✳ *How do I keep others' negative attitudes*
from infecting and affecting my attitude?

✳ *What are my assets – talents, personality traits, fortes?*

✳ *What do I value the most…and why?*

My Notes:

_____

_____

_____

_____

_____

_____

_____

_____

_____

_____

_____

_____

_____

_____

_____

_____

_____

_____

LEADING WITH FAITH FIRST

Then all my other decisions for relationships, in casting votes,
practicing good business ethics, how I treat others
and all the rest – follow second.

Every day I am bombarded with many news snippets from the radio, internet, emails, TV, newspaper headlines and in some conversations. Much of the news is chaotic with media using tactics trying to sway my thinking and advertising to appeal for my dollars. Much is bent-logic looking to get my reaction, emotion and sympathy. Most products are not built to last anymore, customer-service is usually an oxymoron, ethics are changed to suit situations and integrity seems to be a lost art. There is little loyalty between businesses and their customers, employers and employees and few trust our governments – federal, state, county and city.

It can certainly create havoc if I listen and see too much...I simply have to turn it off. The craziness can be from a neighbor just down the street, coming from America's leadership or from around the world. How I spend my time, what I read and listen to and the people I surround myself with will help determine how I believe, think and act.

My faith in God guides my heart to make the best decisions possible. Leading with my faith first is difficult. My principles of faith are usually contrary to what media is hyping and the confusion coming from those who don't believe in God and Jesus Christ. I can choose to ask, *"What would Jesus do?"* and, *"What does the Bible say?"* God is sovereign. The Bible is my road map to living with His standards and truths that are absolute and non-negotiable.

Noah Webster was a soldier, attorney, educator, public official and author. He lived from 1758 to 1843 and is most well-known for writing of *The American Dictionary of the English Language* in 1828. Mr. Webster wrote in *A Collection of Papers on Political, Literary, and Moral Subjects* in 1843, *"The moral principles and precepts contained in the Scriptures ought to form the basis of all our civil constitutions and laws...All the miseries and evils which men suffer from vice, crime, ambition, injustice, oppression, slavery and war, proceed from their despising or neglecting the precepts contained in the Bible."*

Following God's principles as Noah Webster wrote about over 150 years ago is simple, though not easy. In following the Lord I may be laughed at, scoffed, called intolerant or seen as a buffoon. In leading with faith first I save a lot of time, don't worry as much and know that God is in front of me leading my path. My decision – I'm leading with faith first!

In reading Luke 12:22-31, God gives me peace of mind, body, soul and heart.

QUESTIONS TO PONDER?

❋ *What are some key distractions I see frequently that steal my time and wear me down?*

❋ *When I'm alone in my car or elsewhere, what kind of music or talk do I listen to?*

❋ *How much time do I spend daily watching TV, playing video games and tracking social media?*

My Notes:

_____

_____

_____

_____

_____

_____

_____

_____

_____

_____

_____

_____

_____

_____

_____

_____

_____

_____

THREE IS NOT A CROWD

An insurance company's TV ads inspire people to copy their actors' actions but not necessarily buy their products.

There's a 30-second television commercial sponsored by a large insurance company that has been running with the same theme for years. The advertisement shows a person doing an unexpected kind act for a stranger while another person observes the good deed. All three people are strangers and each is blessed by the doing, receiving or watching the giving behavior. The one who watched the good deed then engages another person and performs a favor for them, while another anonymous person watches. The cycle continues with different ads with three separate people each time.

At a neighborhood picnic I learned some friends, Dan and Sandy, were traveling to central Wisconsin. I had just been there a few months before for a family reunion. Casually, I suggested that if they wanted to purchase a case of Point Lager for me, I'd appreciate and pay for it. Nothing was confirmed and a few days later they left on their driving trip.

Some weeks passed and a friend, Mark, asked me to take him to a doctor's appointment for an outpatient procedure. For the early morning appointment, I picked him up from his home and took him to the doctor's office. Being short on cash Mark asked if he could borrow some money from me. The amount in my wallet was sufficient and Mark said he would pay me back at the first of the month. His treatment was completed a few hours later and I drove him home.

That afternoon a business associate, Jerry, came to my home office for an appointment. My office is in the downstairs area of our home and is quietly away from distractions. While Jerry and I were completing some work the phone rang. My neighbors had returned from Wisconsin and Dan said they had a case of beer for me! I asked him how much I owed and he gave me the dollar amount. I suggested that I bring the money by the next day since Mark had depleted all my cash earlier. But Dan wanted to bring the Point Lager then so I said, *"I'll see you in a few minutes."*

When Dan rang our doorbell, I left Jerry in my office. Dan handed me the case of beer and then said, *"You don't owe me any money. When we moved here you were very helpful to us and we appreciate that."* After being positive about his gesture, I thanked Dan for his kindness…and that I was going to enjoy the beer. Then, I related the story about Mark borrowing some money. I told Dan I would be calling Mark the next day. Mark would then learn why he would no longer owe me the cash because of the favor done for me by Dan.

As I entered my office with the case of beer I told Jerry about the borrowed money, the case of beer and that one favor turned into another. Jerry said, *"That's how you are – connecting people and serving them."*

On Tuesday morning I called Mark and said, *"You don't owe me any money because of what Dan did for me."*

Reading Romans 12:9-13, I am reminded that God shows me how to be a Christian in loving my neighbor, friend, fellow saint or enemy.

QUESTIONS TO PONDER?

❋   *How often do I witness serendipity moments and recognize opportunities to fill in the blanks for others?*

❋   *I wonder who sees my actions – good, mediocre and bad – and will they emulate them?*

❋   *From the praises, accolades and stories given by a few, will the rest recognize who they're talking about?*

❋   *What book (not required) am I reading now?*

❋   *And what I'm listening to, reading, viewing and who I'm associating with – are they good for me in the long-term?*

My Notes:

_____

_____

_____

_____

_____

_____

_____

_____

_____

_____

_____

_____

_____

_____

_____

_____

_____

INTEGRITY HAS ONE FACE

Dishonesty, deceit, omission of facts, lying and a myriad of other untruths, constitute fraud and are delivered with many faces.

Integrity – you either have it or you don't. My father's wonderful example of integrity was lived out each day through his law work, home life and other activities. He suggested, that even a hint or look of impropriety, was enough to damage a good name and put ethics into question. At the dinner table each night, he talked about corporate contracts he constructed, details of trips abroad and what had happened that day.

Once, Dad went to the Caribbean Sea on a business trip. One of his colleagues was an attorney and a single woman. After negotiations were done in an office setting all day, everyone retired to their cabana rooms surrounding the outside pool. Dad and the woman attorney needed to wrap up some work details, so she went to his room. As she walked in, Dad propped open the door so all was transparent to everyone. Another time, my father borrowed a T-earth augur from our next door neighbor, Dr. Zook. We bore holes in the ground under a pecan tree in the front yard to fertilize its root system. The auger broke. The neighbor said Dad did not have to buy a new one, but Dad insisted that since he was using it, our neighbor needed to be reimbursed. So, Dad bought Dr. Zook a new auger! Another time, my father conducted an internal investigation of credit card fraud with company cards. When he was ready with the proof, he went to the Victoria, Texas office unannounced. After inviting each employee into a private room, he showed them their signatures on company cards for personal use. Each person denied their culpability and were fired.

On December 5, 2016 my father would have been 100 years old. He lived a few months after his 84th birthday and never lost his resolute desire to do things well, be regarded in high esteem and honor God in His standards. On that same day of Dad's 100th birthday, I was involved in a national conference call led by the Vice President of Sales for the company that employed me. Also on the call were two local colleagues and another 35 sales reps from around the country. The VP of Sales opened with a role call and then moved into a 20-minute presentation with points of fear of loss and creating value with the customer. He then said, *"Everyone likes a good deal, so sell like I do. I never show them the price sheet. I tell them the price is twice what it actually is. And if they buy today, I'll cut the price in half (actual price)."* The VP went on about some other things, but I didn't hear much more. I knew the VP had no integrity and taught bait and switch tactics that are illegal and unethical. After the call ended, one of the local colleagues called me. He had hired me a few weeks before and said, *"I don't do that, and I'm sure you won't either!"* My colleague and I no longer work for the company.

In reading Isaiah 5:20 and II Timothy 4:3,
I better hope that God's ways are my guideposts.

QUESTIONS TO PONDER?

✳ *What's the difference between illegal, unethical and immoral?*

✳ *Ever encountered all three at the same time?*

✳ *When a colleague, family member, friend or a child crosses the line of integrity, how do you initially approach the situation? What is the base of your foundation or moral compass?*

✳ *Do you have integrity in everything you do?*

✳ *Write down three examples of personal and printed broadcast news that had questions of integrity?*

My Notes:

PRACTICING HUMOR, HUMILITY, AND HEART

I am not a big fan of parking meters and believe they actually prevent and discourage business. Following are three examples of reactions to them.

Humor?

On my way to a downtown luncheon, I realized I did not have enough quarters to feed a parking meter. I stopped by a friend's office, who is an attorney, and she lent me two quarters. This was my thank-you letter to her.

Thanks for lending me the two quarters this week. I drove downtown right away and found a parking place on the street a block from my meeting.

When I inserted the quarters into the meter the meter began to flash the message, *"Illegal transaction."* Unfortunately, one of the Colorado Springs meter maids was close by and inquired what I had done. I told her of inserting the two quarters and she said the only time this message appears is when someone has inserted slugs or counterfeit change.

I told her I was unaware of the quarters being anything but legal, but she said she would alert our police department. The meter maid then called the police and a squad car showed up a few minutes later. The policeman said, *"Since you've committed a crime, I have to take you to jail."* I couldn't believe what was happening – paying for a parking meter to attend a business luncheon and then going to jail!

After spending three hours in our downtown jail, I was given my one phone call. My wife was able to post bond to get me out. The fine was $225 including court costs, and I was to appear in court on the following Monday morning. I learned the city's District Attorney had recently issued a statement concerning the consequences of using these slug counterfeit quarters. His statement included that the police department was tracing the origins of these quarters. Since you gave me the slug quarters, I gave the police department your name, office address and phone number. The arresting officer told me that you should expect a police inquiry to follow up with you soon.

Of course, this is all fiction! Hope your heart didn't jump too much and enclosed are *"two good"* quarters to pay you back.   *Charles*

Humility

At my Uncle Marion's funeral, I learned about one of his good habits that served many anonymous people.

My father and Uncle Marion were close and best friends. Two years after Dad died, Uncle Marion succumbed almost eight weeks after his 88th birthday.

At his funeral service, Marion's oldest daughter, Mary, gave part of his eulogy. It was delightful…because I learned some new things about a man who I knew all of my life. The chord that awed me the most about Mary's comments was something that Marion did on most trips to his downtown law office in Beaumont, Texas.

Mary said when she was with her father on those visits to his office, they always parked on the street. He told her he always took all of his spare change, and after filling his parking meter, he would walk down the street and fill other people's meters. Marion did not like parking meters at all! Since he had been doing this practice for many years and was a long-time resident, Beaumont's parking meter police were aware of his actions and did not harass him about it. To their chagrin, the city probably lost a lot of money in parking tickets!

Heart

If I don't feed parking meters, I'll get
$20 tickets. Instead of getting irritated
about the process — I now pay it, don't
park where the meters are posted and/or
do the same thing as my Uncle Marion
did for others.

The City of Colorado Springs has a parking enterprise in the downtown area and on a university campus. It collects parking meter money and fines for tickets paid. I believe it's a racket that deters people from going downtown and hurts the small businesses that depend on new and old customers patronizing them. And, the City then spends millions of dollars each year building new streetscapes funded by the parking enterprise.

Though, I disagree with the tactics of the City's downtown parking system, I know there's not much I can do to change it. What I can do – to *positively change* the outcome of feeding parking meters and getting tickets is the following: • Carry a roll of quarters in my car console; • Thank the meter people for doing their jobs, even though I don't like what they do; • Rarely, do I get tickets now, but when I do, I pay them immediately so that I don't dwell on the irritation of getting the fine; • Explore innovative ways to bolster business so our parking system serves people instead of penalizing them; • Be generous with my change when I see people frantically looking for money to feed their meter; • Act anonymously like Uncle Marion to keep someone from getting a parking ticket! *I've done each of these ideas with favorable results.*

In reading Matthew 6:1-18, I believe the better examples
are conveyed in stories of
Humility and Heart vs. the Humor? story.

QUESTIONS TO PONDER?

❋ *Fortunately, the lawyer who read my Humor? letter took it well after she gasped. Do I let friends and colleagues review correspondence before I post, send or communicate them?*

❋ *What small things can I do to serve someone anonymously, like my Uncle Marion did?*

❋ *Do I practice humility and heart before exercising what I believe is humor?*

My Notes:

FALLING INTO PLACE

On a hike with others, one slip could have resulted in injuries or worse.
Instead, I walked away with only grass stains on my golf shirt.

As a member of the City of Colorado Springs Parks, Recreation
& Cultural Services Advisory Board, I was also appointed for a one-
year term to our Trails, Open Space and Parks (TOPS) Working
Committee. Both are volunteer positions. For the TOPS position, we
occasionally viewed potential property for the city to buy *(part of
our sales tax of $0.01 for every $10.00)*. On one of our hikes, 10 of
us were first driven to a site of vacant land. Maps were passed out
while a short talk was given describing the property. Our 45-minute
adventure was filled with looking up at escarpments, avoiding scree,
crossing a creek several times, seeing a school of fish and viewing
breath-taking scenes into a canyon.

After climbing to the top of a hill, we discussed the attributes
of the possible land acquisition. There wasn't much room for the
10 of us so we crouched together for a picture. Then, in single file
we began descending down the steep slope off the hill. Fortunately,
the person in front of me was not close. My right foot gave way on
a loose rock; my hands broke my fall and I rolled onto my back.
Being a bit stunned, I was then looking upwards to the sky! David,
who was behind me, asked if I was okay. With no twisted muscles or
broken bones, I was only a bit disoriented. One of our guides, Sarah,
then walked with me down an easier route, while the rest hiked down
the steeper way.

The only damage done was to my ego – bruised with some
embarrassment! When I got home, my wife asked, *"Did you hurt the
ground?"*

In reading Psalm 121:1-8, I know whatever happens to me, God is there to guide me through it.

QUESTIONS TO PONDER?

✳ *Do you think I was lucky, in God's protection or what?*

✳ *Ever taken a hike with friends or family in your city, a state park or national park?*

✳ *What kind of adventure could you create for them that doesn't cost much money and only a little time?*

✳ *What memories would be created for a lifetime?*

✳ *How do you react when taken by surprise?*

✳ *Is your first response answered with a cuss word or other expletive?*

✳ *Would you want your wife, girlfriend, mother, sister or children to hear what you said?*

✳ *Does your city have enough open space, parks and trails available for its population?*

✳ *Take the total number of acres of parks and open spaces and divide it by your population. The citizens of Colorado Springs have some of the highest numbers of space available per citizen.*

My Notes:

_____

_____

_____

_____

_____

_____

_____

_____

_____

_____

_____

_____

_____

_____

_____

_____

_____

_____

FLUNKING OUT OF COLLEGE

The path of obtaining my college degree taught me the value of having
purpose, possessing confidence…and just moving forward.

Upon entering Stephen F. Austin State University in Nacogdoches, Texas at age 18, I declared my major as Psychology. A year later, I changed it to Radio Broadcasting. In college life, I had little direction or accountability, no goals and floundered my way through courses with many Cs, some Bs and more Ds than I want to remember. One year into college, I joined a fraternity – it became my real major! Partying was a weekend event that blurred into some weekdays, too. For the weekend nights my drink of choice was beer on Fridays, hard liquor on Saturdays and wine on Sundays.

In beginning my 4th year of college, many friends were close to graduation, while I was nowhere near to earning a Bachelor of Arts degree. Frustrated with my progress, I flunked out that semester with Ds and Fs. Disappointed in what I was doing, I also didn't know the why, where, when, how or what to do next.

First, I moved to my parents' home in Houston and found a temporary oil tool job that lasted for six weeks. With some money saved, I drove 1,500 miles to Canada to visit relatives, see the beautiful countryside and figure out my next move. Though, I stayed with family, I felt like a visitor because of my angst. After four weeks staying there and thinking about what I was going to do with the rest of my life, I decided to drive home to Houston.

After arriving back to the Houston metropolis, I was given a maintenance job working with one of my college fraternity brothers, Jimmy. He was Vice President of a typography business. Then, one of my good friends, David, was in Houston and needed a roommate. My mother knew a minister who was vacating his apartment for the summer. David and I rented the minister's apartment; it was located six blocks from my new job!

I worked the maintenance job mowing lawns, cleaned the office after-hours and did extracurricular activities for some of the management. After nine months, I asked Jimmy if I could do a job that used more of my brain cells!? He promoted me to be a proofreader; I began training right away. Two weeks later, the midnight supervisor quit and I was promoted into his position!

Proofreading typography and camera graphics became a passion. Relishing in my new trade, I learned about typefaces, proofed for typos and began to understand spacing, leading and more. I met clients, enjoyed the relationships with my fellow employees and began to feel more confident and respect for myself. After working the new job for a year, I knew my next move was to return to college and finish a degree. Giving my employer a year's notice granted human resources plenty of time to find a replacement.

I returned to the same college where I started before. Now, I was more mature and ready to study! My priorities changed – before it was partying, now it was to obtain my degree. Since I flunked out of the university three years before, my grade point average was very low with many courses needing to be taken over. I changed my major again – this time to Communications with an emphasis in Journalism and a minor in Political Science. And, I repeated the D and F courses to at least a C grade one by one to fulfill my Bachelor of Arts degree requirements.

A campus dean who had put me on scholastic and disciplinary probation in my first stint in college was now Dean of Housing. Not knowing of his promotion, I visited the office to inquire about on-campus housing. At our impromptu meeting, he granted me an on-campus apartment that was less than a block from classes. To support my way through college, I sold advertising for the college paper…and excelled in that role! I also joined a professional on-campus organization.

Though, I participated with my fraternity in the second stint of college, it was less of a priority than before. A little over two years after returning to college, I graduated with my degree, debt-free and with a 2.3 grade point average (GPA).

When I've spoken to groups of children like Junior Achievement classes, younger adults and individuals – I've reiterated my experience of flunking out of college and the success afterwards. My purpose…is hopefully they don't make the same mistakes I did. And, getting into a masters' program is hard to do with a 2.3 GPA!

In reading Joshua 1:9 and Hebrews 10:35-36, I am blessed to know that God
is watching over me, even if I don't understand who He is or why He cares.

QUESTIONS TO PONDER?

❋   *Know any college students who don't seem to*
have any direction? If so, are you judging them or
looking to meet them where they're at?

❋   *Have you heard the adage, "The C students*
own the companies that the A students work for."?
What do you think of that statement?

❋   *Are you floundering in high school/college/trade*
school, your job or where you are in life now? How
will you change or do something different?

❋   *Why do you think things turned around for*
me? I was not a Christian at the time of gaining
my success in the second stint of college.

❋   *Are you willing to tell others about your mistakes?*

My Notes:

_____

_____

_____

_____

_____

_____

_____

_____

_____

_____

_____

_____

_____

_____

_____

_____

_____

_____

RELATIONSHIP MATTERS

*An employer once announced in a sales meeting, "When you know people
and don't use them, it's worthless." Not agreeing with his viewpoint,
I do believe in utilizing relationships with a servant's
heart – and that's worthwhile!*

*A correlation to this was my privilege in getting to know a
federal Congressman in the Houston area.*

One of my sales jobs was as the membership director of a regional chamber of commerce in the Houston metropolitan area. In
prospecting for new members and networking with the membership,
I met with owners, managers and sales representatives of large companies, small businesses, non-profit organizations and our govern-
ment elected officials.

A United States House of Representatives Congressman relocated his office from the downtown federal building to our south-
west area of Houston. In our first meeting, he decided to join our
chamber of commerce. He said, *"I like being closer to my constituents
– the parking is free for them and I can see out my eye-level windows!"* Right
after joining, he began attending events and getting to know his constituents, as his neighbors.

Being an independent contractor for the chamber and owning a
small company, I was interested in changing our tax codes to benefit
businesses. Our new chamber member, the Congressman, served on
the Budget and Financial Service Committee. He helped craft legislation to modernize banking and securities laws and was actively involved in the drafting and passage of the Balanced Budget Act of
1997. I asked his office for a meeting with myself and some representatives with the local organization of National Retail Sales Tax
(NRST). The meeting was congenial, though the Congressman did
not agree with NRST's approach in changing the Internal Revenue
Service (IRS)'s code of laws. Soon afterwards, I wrote an editorial in
the *Houston Chronicle* about my views in supporting NRST legislation.
About a month later, I was audited by the IRS for one tax year return.

The Congressman and I continued our friendship at chamber events. Our chamber president asked him on occasion to apprise the membership about Congress' progress affecting the business community. About a year after our first NRST meeting, I asked for a second appointment to discuss the same agenda. We did, and the results were the same as before. And, I wrote another editorial in the *Houston Chronicle* for a national retail sales tax. Again, I was audited by the IRS for another tax year return.

Because of our friendship and his service on the Budget and Financial Service Committee, I asked the Congressman's office for an appointment on a personal matter. A few weeks later we met in his office. He said, *"What's up, Charles?"* I related to him my belief of being targeted by the IRS for the content in my editorials – two years in a row. He looked at me and said, *"Write down your social security number on this piece of paper."* I wrote it down and gave it to my friend. He then said, *"You'll never hear from the IRS again."* And, I didn't!

Former Congressman Kenneth Bentsen represented the 25th District of Texas in the United States House of Representatives from 1995 to 2003, serving on the Budget and Financial Services Committees.

During his time in office, he helped craft legislation to modernize American banking and securities laws and helped prepare the nation's response to the Asian financial crisis. He was also actively involved in the drafting and passage of the Balanced Budget Act of 1997 and the Sarbanes-Oxley Act of 2002, which improved federal oversight of U.S. capital markets. Following his time in office, Mr. Bentsen served as a Managing Director of Public Strategies, Inc., a public affairs consulting firm. He then became President of the Equipment Leasing and Finance Association, a national trade association representing financial services companies and manufacturers. After that stint, he became President and CEO of Securities Industry and Financial Markets Association (SIFMA). Born in Houston in 1959, Mr. Bentsen is the nephew of former Texas Senator and Treasury Secretary Lloyd Millard Bentsen, Jr.

In reading Philippians 4:8-9, it's better to strive towards excellence.

QUESTIONS TO PONDER?

✳ *Are you friends with your elected officials,
whether you voted for them or not?*

✳ *Do you know the difference in respecting the person's office,
whether you like the person in the office or not? This is for
elected and appointed national, state, county and city offices.*

✳ *Do you congratulate people for running for office and then
winning the office, even if you didn't support or vote for them?*

✳ *Do you write editorials in a congenial manner
in your local print media? Do you relate information
on social media in a non-confrontational way?*

✳ *After writing a ballistic post, would you be able to sit
down and meet those people in a face-to-face meeting?*

✳ *What does the word, neighbor, mean to you?*

✳ *Instead of focusing on differences you have with
someone, why not focus on the likenesses you have
with them and/or look for common ground?*

✳ *Here's a challenge for you – seek out a person whom you are
at odds with now. Meet, get to know them better and at least land
on something in common. Pray before and after your meeting.*

✳ *Would you set an example for our Congress and other elected
officials by extending your hand across the fence to your neighbor?*

My Notes:

_____

_____

_____

_____

_____

_____

_____

_____

_____

_____

_____

_____

_____

_____

_____

_____

_____

_____

_____

TELL THEM THE TRUTH, MARK!

*While mentoring a man, I watched him shrink the gap between
his old thinking and his new life in Christ.*

E^2 *(Evangelism and Edification squared)* is a term I learned from a local Christian business men's group. The cadre of 200+ men met for
several weekly Bible studies, monthly luncheons, periodic seminars
and once-a-year retreats and breakfasts. The term, E^2, means you are
either evangelizing an unbeliever or edifying a Christian believer. I
attended most of the monthly luncheons and usually invited a friend
or an acquaintance to be my guest.

For one of the luncheons, I did not invite a guest. After arriving
at the restaurant, I found a table and engaged in small talk with some
of the men I knew. One man sitting at my table, Mark, was someone
else's guest. Mark struck up a conversation with me. He was recently
released from prison and was living at a Christian ministry half-way
home. Mark said, *"I need a mentor and will you be the one?"* Being a bit
taken aback, I answered, *"Ask your director if that's okay and I will see
you next month."* The next month rolled around and I went to the
luncheon, again without a guest. Mark was sitting at the same table as
before and said, *"The director said it is okay."* I forgot our previous conversation and asked him, *"What's okay?"* Mark reiterated his question
and my response from the month before. I asked a few perfunctory
questions and realized Mark was taking a big step in changing his life.

Mark and I began to meet on a weekly basis for coffee or lunch.
We discussed the things of God, his walk with Christ and how a
relationship with the Creator would change his thinking. Our study
material included a Bible and a devotional, *Thoughts from the Diary of
a Desperate Man.* The half-way house director was somewhat wary
of our continual meetings. Another man, Don, in our men's group
counseled me with, *"Meet the man where he's at and keep in touch no matter
whether you meet on a regular basis or not."*

The gap, between Mark's old thinking and the application of
God's Word into his life, began to close over time. Week after week,

I saw the *"light bulb"* click on when Mark understood one of God's principles. Mark invited me to meet with his parole officer. During our appointment the lady told me she wished more of their parolees had mentors to walk alongside them during probation and afterwards.

One afternoon, I received a phone call from Mark. He said, *"I let a one of the guys in the half- way house con me."* Mark had rented a car from a local rental agency and let the other guy, an ex- con, drive it all over the area. The ex-con and a girlfriend ran up fees of $800; the agency then debited Mark's checking account. Because there wasn't enough money in his account to cover the rental expenses, other checks bounced for bill payments.

Mark was now in a lot of trouble with the rental agency owner, the Colorado Springs Police Department and his other debtors. He said the agency owner, two police officers and his apartment manager were going to meet him at his apartment the next day at an appointed time. Mark asked, *"Could you come and be here for me?"* For some reason, I could not attend the meeting with the five of them. Mark was desperate and scared. He was afraid, that if he was charged with a crime, he would go back to jail. I said, *"Mark, tell them everything and no matter how bad it sounds or looks, tell them the truth. Tell them, you will pay back everything you owe to the rental agency and the rest of them."* We concluded the phone call with prayer.

The morning after the meeting Mark called me. He said, *"I'm not going to jail! The owner of the car rental agency believed I will pay him back all of it and he's not pressing charges."* The next day I met Mark at his apartment to review the list of 18 businesses he owed money. We prayed over the list and then visited each one. None of them pressed charges against Mark. I suggested he go by each business every month with a payment of at least $5. Even if he did not have the minimum amount to pay, he needed to tell them in person of his intentions. Mark was consistent in his monthly stops to see each of the businesses. The car rental agency owner told him he did not have to come in each month, believing Mark would pay it all back in time.

It took about a year – Mark paid all of the businesses back 100%! The apartment manager also gave him a good reference. From time to time, Mark and I meet for breakfast or lunch. We discuss the things of God, challenges and praises we each are experiencing and how we are serving the Lord. And, many times Mark has poured back into me. Today, you can't tell who's the mentee or the mentor.

In reading II Timothy 2:2 and John 13:34-35, I realize that just having God's Word in me without doing anything with it, may be a disappointment to Him.

QUESTIONS TO PONDER?

❋   *Ever been asked to be a mentor? Or have you offered to be a mentor to someone who needs some direction?*

❋   *I wonder how many prisoners, whether they are in the county jail or serving a life sentence, would benefit from having a mentor. Do you know the statistics of the men and women in prison who come from broken homes?*

❋   *Want to see God at work? Go alongside a man or a woman, follow God's tenets and let Him do the heavy lifting. That's for evangelism or edification – E^2.*

❋   *How many miracles can one person experience?*

❋   *Was Mark just lucky to come through unscathed from his bad choice of lending his rental car?*

My Notes:

_____

_____

_____

_____

_____

_____

_____

_____

_____

_____

_____

_____

_____

_____

_____

_____

EVER STOLEN ANYTHING?

This question was asked on a Securities Exchange Commission questionnaire, and after some thought, I answered "Yes" with a short explanation.

After graduating from high school, I applied to a local movie theater for a summer usher position. The manager hired me to work most night shifts; I stood in one place between the shows. My job was to take the patrons' tickets, tear them in half, hand their stubs back and direct them to which theater their movie was showing.

A girl, JoAnn, about my age was hired at the same time to be an usher, too. Though, she had a boyfriend, I was enamored with her beauty and confidence. While the movies were showing, we talked a lot, spoke with the concessionaire employees and glimpsed into the theaters to see a few of the movie scenes.

Into the job only two weeks, I was bored and got stupid. Instead of tearing two tickets in half, I put them in my pocket. Surmising I would give the tickets to JoAnn, I figured she'd be more interested in me. I gave her both tickets and she accepted them. Apparently, the manager was watching our dishonesty and fired both of us! I was embarrassed, went home and told my parents. In becoming an Eagle Scout the year before, I knew the Scout Law's first point of being *Trustworthy*. In stealing those tickets, I dishonored the promise to be *Trustworthy*, was humbled and moved on. A few days later, I found another job working at a fast-food restaurant. I finished out the summer there, before going to my first semester of college.

Since my two-week stint of working at the movie theater, I've worked many jobs. As with the Securities Exchange Commission and for other job applications, sometimes there's a question, *"Have you ever stolen anything?"* My answer is with a humble *"Yes,"* as I relay my job experience at the movie theater.

*In reading Exodus 20:15 and I John 5:3, it's better to follow God's standard
than to rely on my own wisdom.*

QUESTIONS TO PONDER?

❋   *Have you ever stolen anything, confessed your act
to a friend, family member and/or God?*

❋   *What do you believe are the consequences of
unconfessed sins, such as stealing from another?*

❋   *What does being Trustworthy mean to you?*

❋   *You may not want to admit this…ever done something
stupid because you were "gaga" over a man or a woman?*

❋   *When you are bored – how do you pass the time?*

My Notes:

AFTER I'M DEAD AND GONE

I hope one or more of these short stories have inspired you and warmed your heart.

My childhood was wonderful with parents who greatly cared and gave me the opportunities of Boy Scouts, tutoring when school subjects were amiss, college and traveling in the United States, Canada and Mexico. We went to church every Sunday, I obtained my Eagle Scout and paper routes and restaurant jobs were staples. After graduating from college I moved to Boulder, Colorado and met my wife two weeks later. My career has been in intangible sales with business services; the most enjoyable volunteer work was serving on the Parks, Recreation & Cultural Services Advisory Board of the City of Colorado Springs.

Writing about these non-fiction events is my passion – it makes me fluid in everything else I do! God gave me this gift of writing short stories and it's my legacy. You may be reading these stories long after I am dead and gone; I hope they are timeless in connecting with readers from one generation to the next. *To prepare my steps, I read Psalm 56:10 and Psalm 57:1-2; I hope this for you, too.*

Let's keep in touch! My website is www.inspirationfortheheart.com.

Your comments are appreciated. If you would like us to pray for you, post your prayer on our website or email it to CharlesCastle07@gmail.com. We will pray for you to receive God's direction and wisdom.

If you've enjoyed *Where are the Instructions?* – I suggest you follow the motto of *The Floating Library.* Its idea is: *Upon receiving this book we request that you read it and give it away to someone else. This book then becomes a shelf-less book in The Floating Library.*

Best to you,

Charles H. Castle